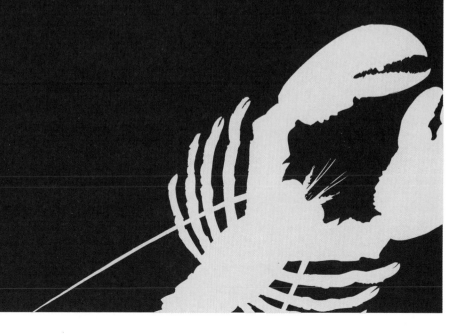

STERLING EPICURE
New York

An Imprint of Sterling Publishing
1166 Avenue of the Americas
New York, NY 10036

ISBN 978-1-4549-1787-8

Distributed in Canada by Sterling Publishing
c/o Canadian Manda Group, 664 Annette Street
Toronto, Ontario, Canada M6S 2C8
Distributed in the United Kingdom by GMC Distribution Services
Castle Place, 166 High Street, Lewes, East Sussex, England BN7 1XU
Distributed in Australia by Capricorn Link (Australia) Pty. Ltd.
P.O. Box 704, Windsor, NSW 2756, Australia

For information about custom editions, special sales, and premium
and corporate purchases, please contact Sterling Special Sales at
800-805-5489 or specialsales@sterlingpublishing.com.

Manufactured in China

Photography by Michael Piazza
Design by Carrie Anne Seaver

2 4 6 8 10 9 7 5 3 1

sterlingpublishing.com

TWO IF BY SEA

DELICIOUS SUSTAINABLE SEAFOOD

STERLING EPICURE
New York

To my lovely *ladyfish*.

CONTENTS

INTRODUCTION

"I ARISE IN THE MORNING TORN BETWEEN A DESIRE TO IMPROVE (OR SAVE) THE WORLD AND A DESIRE TO ENJOY (OR SAVOR) THE WORLD. THIS MAKES IT HARD TO PLAN THE DAY."

—E. B. WHITE

I was one of those little boys whose attention, once trained on a tidal pool, was not to be diverted without a fight. Under a shallow lens of seawater, I discovered an entire world—tiny shrimp and minnows, snails and periwinkles, mussels, hermit crabs, starfish, and more. These creatures were probably unaware of their now limited environment. As a land-bound boy, I was unaware of the unlimited environment from which they had recently been separated.

We are all drawn to nature in our own ways and carry our own fascinations. My curiosity always centered around what things tasted like, what delicious discoveries might be underfoot. Not surprisingly, I became a chef. My discoveries continued as I tasted ingredients from every corner of the globe. I learned about cultures and the traditions they celebrated through food. I let my creativity run wild, combining ingredients from here, there, and everywhere in between and in the process rudely discovered that unchecked creativity can be something of a handicap when it comes to being a good cook. Good cooking is more often an exercise in subtraction than addition, as we learn to strip away any superfluous flavors and reveal just the ingredients of structure, no noise.

So I stepped back, took myself out of the equation, and revisited the ingredients. I began to mine those shore time memories. I was no longer interested in manipulating flavors but in eliciting them. I stopped looking for inspiration in the pages of the latest culinary masterpieces (though I will forever pay respect to that level of craft). I started asking for more details about the food I was serving. I read up on the history of how ingredients had been used long before dinner was

entertainment. I started visiting the people who produced the food I was serving. And I began to see just how narrow my repertoire of food had been.

The fascination that held me rapt to those tide pools began to pull at my creative process. Rather than come up with dishes featuring the same familiar varieties of seafood, I waded around the flavors of the menu. I ventured out to see what expanse I could discover (and into what depths my guests would follow me!).

The diversity I discovered forced me to accept some hard truths about sustainability. Sustainability is an incredibly difficult topic to understand, and efforts to achieve it are often difficult to measure. When it comes to seafood, I believe that supporting domestically produced seafood is one of the surest ways to promote sustainability. The United States' fisheries management policies are the best in the world. I believe if the policies are good and the fishermen follow those policies, then we have a responsibility to support the fishermen. However, it's not enough simply to buy domestic fish; we need to buy a diversity of domestic product.

Brave men and women have for centuries set off from safe harbor to fish. But when they pull their nets on board, today's fishermen are faced with the stark reality that consumers are willing to eat only a few species. Many of the fish they haul up have not found favor at our tables and do not earn fair return for the effort it takes to catch them. Oftentimes these unpopular fish go back overboard. Others that do make it to the dock are so undervalued that they end up as bait or fertilizer. Our demand for a limited array of seafood has brought about a difficult situation. Our oceans have been damaged, fish populations have been depleted, and those diminishing returns have laid to rust a once mighty fishing fleet and the rightly proud communities built from the riches of the sea.

For too long we have told the oceans and fishermen what we are willing to eat, rather than asking them what they can supply. What the oceans can provide is far more diverse and interesting than what our limited palates demand. Recently there has been a lot of conversation about this very topic—while the health of our ecosystems needs to be monitored through rigorous scientific methods, so too must we look at our civic responsibility in the role of fisheries. We can't forget that fisheries are economic systems that employ men and women who put food on our tables while upholding generations of heritage and tradition.

When we understand fishing to be a noble pursuit, like farming, we begin to apply a larger set of values to seafood as part of the food system. We can begin to see our recipes and our shopping choices as part of our good faith effort to make a better future. This way of thinking is admittedly an evolution of what I have advocated previously. For too long we have only looked to the fishermen as the bad actors. They are not bad actors. The consumer is not a bad actor. But the consumer and the fisherman are so disconnected that they cannot act together to create rational economic systems. Rational systems produce foods such as farmed salmon, an industry worth supporting because it is constantly progressing toward more environmentally sustainable operations. And we must even lend support to species that may be on the "red" list. In my opinion, the very best way to save a species is to interact with that species. And the most charismatic species that we need to save is indeed the fishermen. By broadening our definition of sustainability to include the seafood systems

that employ and feed people and that enable enduring and thriving communities, we ultimately achieve the true goal of sustainability: we preserve and continue the story of our relationship with the oceans through the food on our plate.

When I was running my Washington, DC, restaurants, my team and I were interacting with fishermen on a daily basis, buying and studying whatever they were able to catch. I bore witness to the enterprise of fishing and the nets hauled aboard, brimming with flavors taken from a far broader circumstance. When opening seafood deliveries shipped from all over the coastal world, our first task was to consult our field guides, playing amateur ichthyologist. When dealing with boats directly, we received exactly what the fishermen pulled from the waters, and in that mix there could be unexpected treats, rare finds, or even completely unknown species. With time and experience, we were able to identify visual markers that offered clues to the character of any given fish. The key is to focus on the small details. We looked to the size, body shape, skin, scales, distribution and number of fins, orientation of eyes, and so on. It was a point of pride for many of my staff to spy a whole fish from a dozen yards away and accurately describe its texture and fat content, offer appropriate cooking methods, determine if the skin is best served on or should be removed after cooking, in addition to a host of other details about that fish's unique culinary personality.

We learned to see unfamiliar species through the lens of known culinary categories. For example, members of the mackerel family, whether it be a Spanish mackerel, the more delicate Boston, or a majestic wahoo, all share sleek, dart-like bodies, short pectoral fins, Mohawk-like dorsal fins, and powerful tails. These pack hunters are vigorous, ever moving, and full flavored. Even if we didn't know immediately what kind of mackerel was on the ice in front of us, we knew it would be delicious grilled and anointed with rosemary-scented butter.

In this book I discuss a number of cooking techniques, all of which are applicable to a host of species. I include recipes for a number of familiar and unfamiliar species, with the hopes that you will find a point of inspiration from which to begin your explorations into the world of seafood. If we demand the red snapper called for by a recipe, we will go home with that fish regardless of its freshness. In our slavish devotion to a recipe, we forget to stop and smell the porgy. If a sheepshead glistens with sea brine and is still stiff with vitality, then please, please buy it! Guess what? It cooks almost exactly like the snapper called for in your recipe. If the swordfish you set out to get is eclipsed by the rosy hue of fresh albacore steaks, then by all means shift your attentions, but don't feel you need to dramatically alter your recipe.

Great-quality seafood deserves to be left alone. There is nothing we can do to improve upon the quality of a pristine piece of fish, so good cooking should just provide a little context for the personality of the raw ingredient. I prefer to employ ingredients that accentuate flavors rather than mask or overpower them, in the form of acid such as citrus and vinegar, simple seasonings such as mace and fresh herbs, and smoke, especially that from lighter, more aromatic woods (cherry, alder, apple, peach).

Now, for cod's sake, I live on the coast of Maine, just up the road from a working waterfront where all kinds of fish are landed. From my backyard, where I raise chickens and harvest eggs and vegetables, I often find opportunity to trade products with fishermen as they pass my house with the day's catch. I understand full well that most people to do not have such access to just landed seafood, but that does not prevent you from accomplishing memorable and incredible meals. Great-quality seafood is now available everywhere. Traditional grocery stores and retail outlets have made incredible strides in improving the quality of their offerings.

However, what I find still needs to be developed is connectivity. We take pride in knowing the place, producer, and provenance of our fruits, vegetables, eggs, meats, wines, and beer. There has been an explosion of farmers markets in our culture, and recognizing the role that farmers play in our society is all but demanded in today's conversations of good cooking. We need to apply this sense of pride to the seafood that we eat. When it comes to the fish on my table, regardless of where it comes from and where I purchased it, I demand that it come with a story. Because ultimately it is storied seafood that connects us to the producer, which, in turn, better ensures sustainability and, quite frankly, the quality and freshness our hard-earned dollars demand.

And hey, what's the best part of fishing? It's not catching the fish; it's telling the tale of catching the fish. The same is true with any meal. The greatest joy of food is in gathering around the table. And though we may not tell tales of fish caught, or the one that got away, we certainly gather to tell stories about our day, our experiences, and the things that matter to us. Storied seafood not only links us to a place or a product, it connects us to the people with whom we are so fortunate to share our meals. And with that in mind, let's start cooking.

Pepper-Allspice Blend

Black pepper is a misused ingredient. Its piquant, animated flavor is not well suited to every dish, but it finds its way into almost every meal, often by habit than by thoughtful application. And, in many cases, the pepper used by home cooks has suffered prolonged cabinet captivity, languishing long enough to diminish its charisma.

Part of the problem is that pepper is too often applied at the wrong time. Salt, added prior to cooking, penetrates the food, accentuating and strengthening its flavors. Used at the same point, pepper sits on top without substantial interaction with the ingredient. Plus, the exposed spice is now at risk of burning. Instead, pepper should be freshly ground over foods just as they are served. This also adds a level of control as you can add pepper to taste, as opposed to hoping you (or the cook) applied the right amount at the beginning of the process. I feel that, in general, pepper alone competes with the clarity of fresh seafood. But I have found that when you pair it with warm, beguiling allspice, pepper's aggressive tones are softened into an incredibly elegant accent. Though most often considered a baking spice, allspice serves a prominent role in savory cooking, too (for instance, it is one of the defining seasonings of Jamaican jerk chicken). When mixed in equal parts with pepper and freshly ground, allspice calms the tone of pepper and implies a hint of the exotic.

Throughout this book, you will see me call for freshly ground pepper-allspice, in place of black pepper. You need no special equipment to create this blend: simply mix equal parts of the two spices and add to a regular pepper grinder. Use this pairing beyond seafood—you'll find it adds a welcome twist to all of your cooking.

Chile Peppers

Gently spiced chiles are as welcome with fish as is lemon. In sauces or stews, I prefer to add Mediterranean varieties, such as Arbol or Calabrian. The bright sweetness of a fresh mild pepper, such as serrano, Fresno, or ají amarillo, adds incredible complexity and balance to a potently acidic dish like ceviche. Ground dried peppers are best used in moderation, sprinkled on fillets to be baked, broiled, or sautéed; Aleppo, Espelette, and traditional red chile flakes are particularly well suited to the briny flavors of fish. In the following recipes, you'll notice the recurring use of smoked sweet paprika, the darling of my spice rack. This sun-dried, slow-smoked sweet pepper known as *pimentón dulce* is almost universally complementary to foods, adding rich color and the specter of rustic smoke flavor. Chiles in all forms are best introduced in the presence of fat (oil or butter), as the flavors bloom and are more evenly distributed throughout a dish.

Fennel in Seafood Cookery

Cool and refreshing, anise-scented fennel is a most flattering partner for all briny, sea-sweet seafood. Long a staple in the sun-drenched cuisines of the Mediterranean and temperate coastlines everywhere, the entire plant is useful. The bulb can be added raw to salads, sautéed, braised in butter, simmered into sauces, or added to stews. When grilling, I like to make a raft of fennel stalks on which to cook fish; the heat imparts a haunting herbal whisper to the seafood. The frilly fronds can be used like an herb and added to salads. As a partner to smoked seafood, fennel knows no equal: its affable personality cuts through and smooths the rustic smoke.

I often choose to use fennel in place of celery and sometimes onions. Each complement fish in its own way, but onions can sometimes add too much bite or sweetness, while highly aromatic celery can overwhelm the subtle flavors of seafood. Fennel, sliced like an onion or diced, imparts a more delicate backdrop and adds complexity and richness to a dish. When cooked, fennel's texture resembles that of both onions and celery.

There is a long tradition of aperitif liquors flavored with anise or fennel, including Pernod®, pastis, vermouths, absinthe, and, my favorite, the New Orleans staple Herbsaint®. Any of these make for a wonderful afternoon respite served chilled alongside cold seafood dishes. I use these elegant liquors to spike vinaigrettes, deglaze a pan for a quick sauce, or sprinkle over a finished dish. I like to brush seafood with Pernod just before grilling (of course, taking a small shot for myself, too).

Mace, the Seafood Spice

Mace is the crimson-bright lacy hull that covers the nutmeg seed. The delicate mace is removed, dried, and most often sold ground. When found whole, it is an intricately twisted, woody bodice, one of the most beautiful of all culinary ingredients. Its fragility makes it difficult to grate, as it yields uneven pieces and constant cuts to your fingertips.

Ground mace, when used promptly after opening, has an exotic scent that is similar to nutmeg, but with its own unique, curious blend of burned cinnamon, anise, blossoming lilies, and Madeira-like nuttiness. Mace doesn't categorize neatly, and is equally at home in sweet and savory applications, such as stews, chowders, spice blends, vinaigrettes, and marinades. Its musky, piquant qualities pair especially well with fuller flavored seafood—think shrimp, salmon, and bluefish. While many assertive spices often debate against seafood, mace yields in agreement.

Mace makes a particularly good addition to salt and spice when curing gravlax or making a brine for fish to be smoked. The spice's heady nature also works well when lightly sprinkled over highly flavored dishes such as ceviche or vinegar-spiked salads just before serving. Its flavor is nicely tamed when combined with dairy, as in a béchamel sauce When I cook with mace, I am often met with curious questions. "Such an interesting flavor . . . what is it?" To which I respond, "It's but an old friend."

The Importance of a Good Cutting Board

The first rule they teach you in culinary school is a simple phrase, *mise en place*, a French term that roughly translates to "everything in its place." It is basically a culinary version of the Boy Scouts' motto of "Be prepared." When cooking, it's important that you enjoy the process, and the best way to do so is to have a plan of action. To keep organized and focused, simply arrange all of your needed ingredients so you know where to find everything.

When I was training line cooks on a new station or initiating them onto the hotline I had a tactic that never failed to instill the importance of good organization. I would ask them to set up their station as if they were heading into the battle of a Saturday night shift. I would then duct tape one of their feet to the floor. The goal was to perform every action required on that station and to reach every ingredient in their *mise* without shifting their taped-down foot.

In my home kitchen, a giant cutting board serves as the mother ship for all cooking operations. I use a giant **Boos Block®** cutting board, one large enough to fillet even the biggest fish I could hope to catch. I chose a maple cutting board for its antimicrobial properties. It has more than enough space to hold all the ingredients I will use for any given meal, and when I plan it out right, I can cook dinner without failing my own tape test. Admittedly I fail more often than not, but it's a fun challenge nonetheless.

I treat my board with the same care as I treat my knives. It's kept well oiled to ensure it doesn't dry out or retain aromas. Through years of constant and careful use its well-worn patina has become an integral part of the personality of my kitchen.

My Go-To Kitchen Equipment

It is said that a good craftsman never blames his tools. I think that the
continuation of that statement is that a good craftsman knows how
to pick great tools. Could all of us manage to get dinner on the table
if given less-than-optimal tools? Yes! We craftsmen soldier on. But it's
well worth making a few smart investments and outfitting your kitchen
with a few tools that make cooking less challenging and more fun. For
instance, the delicate and precise surgery of filleting fish is best accom-
plished with a well-sharpened knife designed for the task. Safely opening an oyster, aka "food inside a rock," requires an oyster knife. Without
one, I wish you good luck in keeping all five of your fingers, my friend.
And when making sauces such as a ginger-herb pesto, it is important to
process the ingredients as efficiently as possible so as to maintain their
fresh and vibrant character. My Vita-Prep® blender has been a constant
workhorse over the years. The pan I reach for more than any other is a
10-inch professional-grade nonstick Zwilling J. A. Henckels® sauté pan.
Its thick bottom retains heat as well as a cast iron skillet, and it is sensi-
tive enough to cook crêpes at a consistent low temperature. I have yet to
succeed in getting a piece of fish to stick. Omelets flip so easily that one
might think I'm a pro. I am all for the myth of the self-made man, the
provider of all needs. I am also happy to have expertly crafted tools to
help me look good under pressure.

APPETIZERS

When I head out to the fish market I tend to bring home more varieties of seafood than my wife thinks is reasonable. This is mostly due to my overeager palate. Other times the fishmonger will hold for me a particular rarity, maybe a single fish that swam into the wrong basket. Such variety is the joy of seafood. I might say that beef is like a one-man play, whereas seafood is a full ensemble Broadway show. The opening act should be highly flavored—these dishes start your meal off with some personality. Big flavors can dull or become muted if not doled out with reserve; a few small bites featuring ingredients that challenge the seafood are a great place to start.

Oysters

REGIONAL FLAVORS

Every oyster is a reflection of its origin. The salinity and brackishness of the water, the quantity of nutrients, the strength of the tides, the depth of the water—every one of these details is part of the tasty tale the oyster tells when you eat it. That said, there are some regional commonalities that apply when shopping for oysters.

Almost all East Coast oysters are of the same species, *Crassostrea virginica*, and these oysters tend to be quite briny, increasingly so the farther north one goes. They may exhibit a range of flavors, from strong minerality and crisp acidity to hints of butter, melon, and coriander, to name just a few.

Multiple oyster species are grown on the West Coast, including the Pacific, Kumamoto, and Olympia. These oysters tend to exhibit more intense flavors than their East Coast counterparts. They have a notable sweetness and common notes of cucumber, melon, copper, and seaweed.

Southern oysters (those coming from south of the Chesapeake Bay and throughout the Gulf of Mexico) tend to have a softer texture and less brine than their other coastal counterparts. The warmer waters of the southerly coast allow the oysters to grow rapidly, and they are often quite a bit larger than cold-water oysters. There is a rich culinary tradition of serving these oysters roasted, broiled, grilled, fried … well, hell, any which way you can, including shucked. I don't mean to pick any fights here, but the southern oyster is, in my opinion, the best suited of the American oysters to provide superior platform for such classic dishes as oysters Rockefeller and oysters Bienville.

Lime and Oysters

Of all of the places to experience an oyster revelation, Lake George, New York, was not my expected road to Damascus. I was listening to Rowan Jacobsen discussing his brilliant book *A Geography of Oysters*, and in a moment of candid side conversation, he revealed that he likes to elevate his oysters with a squeeze of fresh lime juice. He believes limes, which are slightly more acidic and floral scented than lemons, better complement oysters, which have more vegetal than fruity notes (think cucumber). West Coast oysters exhibit this affinity more than their East Coast comrades, due to their more concentrated personalities. Many purists may exhibit aggressive behavior should this topic come up for debate, but I believe that a simple taste test will tame tempers and open minds—while it may not be right for them, it's also not wrong.

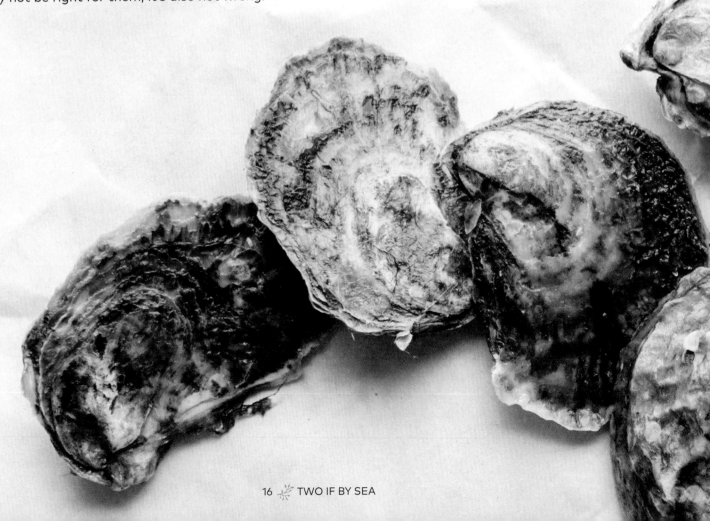

How to Make Crushed Ice

When serving clams and oysters on the half-shell, you want to keep them as cold as is possible. Crushed ice lets you nestle the shells into the icy chill, and it helps to keep them upright, so you don't lose a drop of their delicious briny juices. Crushed ice is easy to make: simply wrap regular ice cubes in a towel and beat them with a wooden rolling pin until they are mostly crushed. Crushed ice will melt pretty quickly, so it's best to platter up the ice and the oysters immediately. This is also perfect ice for many cocktails.

SAUCING THE OYSTER

Raw shellfish has a long tradition of accompaniments, including cocktail sauce, lemon juice, horseradish, and the French sauce known as mignonette. Mignonette is a mixture of vinegar and water flavored with freshly diced shallot and peppercorn. The peppery bite, sweet shallot, and bright acidity of the vinegar enlivens oysters, especially those that are super briny and need a bit of balance. Here I present a couple of different mignonette recipes: and a traditional one best paired with East Coast oysters, and a creative take that plays well with the oysters of our West Coast.

SPICY WEST COAST MIGNONETTE

MAKES ENOUGH FOR 1 TO 2 DOZEN OYSTERS

2 tablespoons minced shallot, rinsed briefly under cold water

3 to 5 thin slices medium-spicy fresh chile pepper, such as Fresno or serrano

3 thin slices fresh ginger

4 turns ground pepper-allspice

Salt

3 tablespoons red wine vinegar

A few drops freshly squeezed lime juice

1 tablespoon finely chopped fresh cilantro

1½ teaspoons chopped fresh tarragon

1 tablespoon water

Combine the shallots, chile pepper, ginger, pepper–allspice, and a pinch of salt with the vinegar and lime juice. Allow the mixture to sit for at least 10 minutes.

Before serving, remove the ginger and chile pepper. Stir in the cilantro and tarragon and add the water to balance the acidity of the sauce. Serve alongside freshly shucked oysters and spoon over them just prior to eating. Use the sauce within 2 hours.

CLASSIC MIGNONETTE

MAKES ENOUGH FOR 1 TO 2 DOZEN OYSTERS

2 tablespoons minced shallot, rinsed briefly under cold water

4 turns coarsely ground pepper-allspice

Salt

3 tablespoons red wine vinegar

2 thin slices ginger (optional)

1 tablespoon water

Combine the shallots, pepper-allspice, and a pinch of salt with the vinegar. If using the ginger, add it so that it is submerged in the vinegar. Allow the mixture to sit for at least 10 minutes.

Before serving, remove the ginger and add the water to balance the acidity of the sauce. Serve alongside freshly shucked oysters and spoon over them just prior to eating. Use the sauce within 2 hours.

BROILED OYSTERS ROCKEFELLER

SERVES 4 TO 6

One of the great American dishes, oysters Rockefeller, was created at Antoine's, the legendary restaurant in New Orleans, and was so named because it was said to be "as rich as Rockefeller." I wanted to work up a lighter, more modern homage, but as I tested recipes, I came to accept that the richness of the classic preparation is indeed something to be cherished. Is it rich? Yes. Is it too rich? Possibly, but you can tweak that. Is it an absolute treat, easy to prepare at home, sophisticated, and in itself a special occasion? A billion times, yes.

24 large oysters

2 bunches watercress, trimmed

1 bunch scallions

½ bunch flat-leaf parsley

16 tablespoons (2 sticks) unsalted butter, divided use

2 teaspoons smoked sweet paprika

A large pinch ground mace

Salt

1 cup heavy cream

4 capfuls Pernod, Herbsaint, or pastis

2 tablespoons Worcestershire sauce

1 to 2 cups panko

Crusty bread, sliced

Lemon wedges

Preheat the broiler to 400°F (or medium high). Line an ovenproof tray with rock salt or folded aluminum foil.

Shuck the oysters and discard the top shell. Drain the liquor, reserving 1 cup of it, and arrange the shucked oysters in their shells on the lined tray.

Bring a pot of gently salted water to a boil. Briefly plunge the watercress, scallions, and parsley in the water to wilt them. Drain well and, using your hands, lightly squeeze as much moisture from them as possible. Finely mince the greens and set them aside.

Heat 8 tablespoons (1 stick) of the butter in a sauté pan over medium heat. Stir the paprika and mace into the butter, toasting the spices until they release their aromas, about 2 minutes. Add the minced greens and a judicious pinch of salt and continue to cook until the greens have warmed through, about 3 minutes.

Add the cream, Pernod, Worcestershire sauce, and the reserved oyster liquor, stirring to combine over high heat. Cook until the liquid has begun to thicken, about 5 minutes.

Meanwhile, cut the remaining 8 tablespoons (1 stick) of butter into small pieces.

Remove the sauce from the heat, let cool a minute or two, then whisk in the remaining butter, one piece at a time, until you have a thick, emulsified mixture.

Let cool to room temperature.

Divide the sauce evenly among the oysters, then sprinkle the bread crumbs over each oyster. (I like just a few crumbs scattered over each, but I leave this up to you.)

Place the tray on the middle rack of the oven and broil until the sauce and liquor in the oysters begin to bubble, 5 to 7 minutes. Move the tray to the top rack and broil another 3 to 5 minutes to cook the oysters through, brown the tops, and crisp the breadcrumbs. (Pay close attention to this step: the crumbs can go from browned to burned in a flash. I suggest cooking this last stage with the oven door cracked open and that you keep your attention directed to the task.) The oysters are fully cooked when they are hot throughout and their edges have curled away from the shell.

Serve piping hot from the oven with crusty bread and lemon wedges, if desired. In my kitchen, these oysters are always accompanied by glasses of ice-cold Pernod.

BROILED OYSTERS
WITH ANCHOVY-ALMOND BUTTER

SERVES 4 TO 6

Almonds take on a nice crunch and char under the broiler, and anchovy boosts the briny sweetness of these buttery oysters. I like to serve them with a dry amontillado sherry or off-dry Sercial Madeira.

24 large oysters, shucked, on the half shell, with liquor drained and reserved

3 recipes Anchovy Butter (page 236), softened

½ cup slivered almonds, crushed nearly to a paste

2 tablespoons chopped flat-leaf parsley

2 teaspoons finely grated orange zest

Crusty bread, sliced

Preheat the broiler to high. Line an ovenproof tray with rock salt or folded aluminum foil.

Shuck the oysters and discard the top shell. Drain and reserve the liquor, and arrange the shucked oysters in their shells on the lined tray.

Combine the anchovy butter, almonds, parsley, orange zest, and up to 3 tablespoons of the reserved oyster liquor in a small bowl and mix well. Spoon a generous dollop of seasoned butter on each oyster.

Place the tray on the top rack of the oven and broil until the butter is bubbling, the almonds are toasted and aromatic, and the edges of the oysters have curled in their shells. Remove from the broiler and serve immediately with crusty bread.

SEAFOOD FOR CEVICHE

Ceviches have a history ranging the world over. The preparations vary greatly (as do the pronunciations and spellings), but all ceviches start with fresh seafood that is marinated in acids and aromatics. The ceviches of South America, including the justly famous versions from Peru, are often made with lime, onion, and herbs, yielding a dish that is at once bracing and refreshing. European versions of marinated seafood tend toward vinegar bases and can include dishes such as marinated poached shellfish, flavored with smoked paprika and cool coriander.

If there are fresh herbs in the marinade, I like to add balance with a red chile pepper, especially my favorite Fresno chile. With a citrus-marinated ceviche, namely those of Peruvian inspiration, I serve it garnished with slices of sweet potato that have been boiled with orange zest and thyme. When serving any style of ceviche, I like to add a bit of texture on the side, best introduced with thin slices of sour apple, endive, bitter radicchio, or frisée.

Another dish with a lengthy and diverse history is escabeche—seafood that has been breaded and fried then marinated with vinegar, aromatic vegetables, garlic, and warm spices, such as cinnamon and cloves. In one of my literary explorations into the history of seafood cooking, I found a recipe for marinated herrings seasoned with a quantity of clove, juniper, mace, and pepper that near equaled the amount of fish. The recipe was recorded centuries prior to the advent of refrigeration, so I suppose this was a method of disguising poor-quality or overly aged fish. Maybe it was an awesome and long forgotten preparation? A faded trend? I'll try it some day. I might be missing out.

SCALLOP CEVICHE
WITH FENNEL AND MINT

SERVES 4

1 pound bay scallops (or small sea scallops, sliced or cut in half)

1 clove garlic, halved

1 slice fresh ginger

1½ cups fresh lime juice

1 small fresh chile pepper, such as Fresno or serrano, finely diced

Salt

2 stalks celery, diced

1 large red onion, thinly sliced (about 2 cups), rinsed briefly under cold water

½ cup very thinly sliced fennel and/or fennel fronds (or a dash of anise-flavored liquor, such as Pernod or anisette)

3 scallions, thinly sliced

2 tablespoons mint leaves, torn into small pieces

1 teaspoon grated mace

Endive, radicchio, and/or boiled sweet potatoes, for serving

Pick through the scallops to remove any remaining bits of shell. Do not wash them.

Rub the sides of a bowl with the garlic and fresh ginger to aromatize it then discard. Add the lime juice, chile, and salt to taste. Stir to dissolve the salt and let sit for a minute.

Add the celery, onion, and fennel (or liquor if using) and toss to coat with the lime juice. Add the scallops and gently toss to mix. Refrigerate for 30 minutes.

Add the scallions, mint, and mace, and toss to combine. Let sit another 3 to 5 minutes and then divide among individual dishes. Spoon any remaining marinade over the dishes and serve immediately with slices of endive, radicchio, and/or boiled sweet potatoes.

SALMON CEVICHE WITH DILL

1¼ pounds salmon, skinned and blood line removed, diced into ½-inch pieces

Salt

1 clove garlic, halved

1 slice fresh ginger

1¼ cups fresh lime juice

¼ cup sherry vinegar

1 fresh chile pepper, such as Fresno or serrano, very thinly sliced or cut into batons

2 teaspoons dried oregano

1 large red onion, very thinly sliced (about 2 cups) and rinsed briefly under cold water

2 stalks celery, thinly sliced

4 tablespoons chopped fresh dill

Nutmeg

Lightly season the diced salmon with salt and let sit for about 5 minutes. Dip the fish in a bowl of cold water to rinse off the salt. Pat dry.

Rub the sides of a bowl with the garlic and fresh ginger to aromatize it; drop the garlic and ginger into the bowl. Add the lime juice, vinegar, chile, and oregano, and season with salt. Stir to dissolve the salt and let sit for 5 minutes.

Remove the garlic and ginger and discard. Add the salmon and toss to thoroughly coat. Let sit 15 minutes.

Add the onion and mix well, taking care not to break up the fish. Let sit for 5 minutes.

Add the celery and dill. Toss to combine and divide among individual dishes, spooning any remaining juices over the dishes. Grate some nutmeg over the top of each dish and serve immediately.

WHITE FISH CEVICHE
WITH ALMONDS AND CURRANTS

SERVES 4

1 pound white fish, such as flounder, grouper, or corvina, skinned and diced into ½-inch pieces

Salt

1 slice fresh ginger

1 clove garlic, halved

1½ cups fresh lime juice

4 tablespoons almonds, toasted

3 tablespoons dried currants or raisins

1 fresh chile pepper, such Fresno or serrano, very thinly sliced

1 large red onion, very thinly sliced (about 2 cups), rinsed briefly under cold water

1 cup loosely packed chervil leaves

Lightly season the diced fish with salt and let sit for about 5 minutes. Dip the fish in a bowl of cold water to rinse off the salt. Pat dry.

Rub the sides of a bowl with the ginger and garlic to aromatize it and discard. Add the lime juice, almonds, currants, chile, and a pinch of salt. Stir to dissolve the salt and let sit for 5 minutes.

Add the fish and toss to coat. Refrigerate for 10 to 15 minutes.

Add the onion and mix well, taking care not to break up the fish. Refrigerate for 5 minutes.

Add half of the chervil and toss to combine. Divide among individual dishes and spoon any remaining juices over the dishes. Garnish each plate with a tuft of the remaining chervil.

SHELLFISH CEVICHE WITH SHERRY

SERVES 4 TO 8

2 pounds mixed shellfish, such as octopus, shrimp, squid, and lobster

1 clove garlic, halved

1 slice fresh ginger

1 cup fresh lime juice

¼ cup sherry vinegar

1 chipotle pepper (or rehydrated Nora pepper), chopped

Salt

1 large red onion, very thinly sliced (about 2 cups) and rinsed briefly under cold water

4 stalks celery, very thinly sliced (about 1 cup)

3 tablespoons Manzanilla or amontillado sherry

3 tablespoons chopped fresh cilantro

Radicchio and boiled sweet potato slices, for serving

Deep-poach all of the shellfish, one variety at a time, in a pot of salted water. If using shrimp or lobster, cook those first, as they will flavor the water for the remaining seafood. Cook until each is barely done, then remove and allow to cool. (See page 186 for information about deep poaching.) Once all of the seafood has been cooked, remove the meats from the shells and cut into bite-size pieces. Reserve the seafood and ½ cup of the cooking liquid.

Rub the sides of a bowl with the garlic and ginger to aromatize it and discard. Add the lime juice, vinegar, chipotle, and a good pinch of salt. Whisk to dissolve the salt and mash the chipotle until it is well mixed with the liquid. Let sit for 5 minutes.

Add the reserved seafood, onion, and celery and toss to combine. Refrigerate for at least 20 minutes and up to 2 hours.

Just before serving, add the sherry and cilantro and toss well. Divide among individual serving dishes and garnish with boiled sweet potato slices and radicchio.

Note: Strained, this marinade makes a particularly good chaser to shots of cold tequila!

Seafood Safety Tips

The proliferation of sushi in this country has tempered our cultural taboos against raw seafood, but we still need to maintain some vigilance to mitigate the risk of foodborne illness. First precaution, as with all seafood: always, always, always buy the freshest, most pristine, most beautiful seafood you can, from the most trusted fishmonger you can find. Avoiding bacteria is mostly about proper handling of seafood throughout the supply chain. Seafood-borne parasites pose another risk, and these can be a little harder to identify. Ask your fishmonger about any potential dangers from parasites, and seek out seafood that has been properly frozen, which kills the parasites.

FRIED SABLEFISH IN SAFFRON-SCENTED ESCABECHE

SERVES 4

When I first encountered this dish in a tiny bar in a forgotten part of Spain, I thought the cook must be confused. Why would somebody go to the trouble of frying all of these little pieces of fish only to drown them in marinade and serve them at room temperature, no less? As is the habit of any self-respecting culinarian, I immediately ordered up a double. As the proprietor expertly portioned out a perfect plate, I realized this was no mistake. The little fingers of crisp-fried fish absorb the harmonious flavors of the sauce—the saffron-scented vinegar, olive oil, and spices—and the mouthfeel is equally wonderful, as the fish's crust helps emulsify the marinade, leading to a richly textured bite.

This recipe is delicious with almost any type of full-flavored fish. I especially like dressed smelts, bluefish, dogfish, albacore tuna, and mackerel. I call for the fish to be salted before being cooked in order to firm up the flesh, which is especially important for flaky white flesh fish like sablefish.

This escabeche is best served at room temperature with lots of crusty, toasty bread and ice-cold glasses of light white wine such as Vinho Verde.

1¼ pounds sablefish, skin and bones removed

Salt

2 cups peanut oil, for frying

1 cup fine cornmeal

½ cup extra-virgin olive oil

2 large onions, thinly sliced from top to bottom

1 large fennel bulb (fronds discarded), thinly sliced

4 cloves garlic, thinly sliced

8 sprigs fresh thyme

4 sprigs fresh oregano or 1 teaspoon dried oregano

4 dried chiles, such as árbol or Calabrian

1 good pinch saffron (10 to 12 threads)

1 cup white wine

1 cup red wine vinegar

Juice of 2 lemons

Cut the fish on a bias into 2-inch-thick strips, season generously with salt, and let sit for 10 to 20 minutes.

Heat the peanut oil in a large pan until it reaches 350°F on a deep-fry thermometer. (For more on frying, see page 192.) Working in three batches, dredge the fish pieces in the cornmeal, making sure they are evenly coated. Carefully place the first batch, one at a time, into the hot oil. Cook, undisturbed, until the pieces develop an even, dark golden crust, 2 to 4 minutes. Remove from the oil and place on a plate lined with paper towels. Repeat until all the fish is cooked.

In a large sauté pan over medium-high heat, combine the olive oil with the onion, fennel, and garlic, and cook until the garlic loses its raw smell, 3 to 5 minutes. Stir in the thyme, oregano, chiles, and saffron, and cook until the saffron is toasted, about 2 minutes. Add the wine and vinegar, season with salt, and bring the sauce to boil. Cook 1 minute more, then remove from the heat.

Place the fried fish in a casserole dish just large enough to hold all the pieces. Pour the still-hot sauce over the fish, nestling the vegetables in and around the fish. The dish should be made at least a few hours ahead. Just before serving, sprinkle the lemon juice over the dish to revive the flavors.

MONKFISH EN ADOBO

SERVES 4

I first enjoyed this classic tapas dish when I was traveling through northern Spain. With its blend of sour, smoky, and sweet flavors, the marinade is potent, and that's the point. The cornmeal crisps quickly and punctuates the savor of the fish with a well-developed crunch. I like to cut the fish in large slices rather than cubes, so there is more surface area and thus more texture. The herb salad provides a refreshing foil to the bites of fried fish and rich aioli. This is food to serve on a large platter and eat with your fingers while you drink ice-cold lagers.

The fish used in this preparation is traditionally dense, having a texture akin to steak when raw. I have used monkfish, sturgeon, amberjack, catfish, and even a mixture of various fish tail and trim pieces, but delicate but well-flavored varieties, such as sablefish or bluefish, also work well in this recipe. As in any good seafood recipe, buy what is freshest and looks best.

1¼ pounds monkfish
loins

Salt

3 cloves garlic, smashed

1 cup water

½ cup sherry vinegar

1 tablespoon
dried oregano

1 tablespoon smoked
sweet paprika

1 tablespoon kosher salt

1 quart peanut oil, for
frying

1½ cups fine cornmeal

1 cup Classic Aioli
(page 257)

½ bunch flat-leaf
parsley, leaves only

6 sprigs mint, leaves
only, torn into
small pieces

1 serrano or Fresno
pepper, thinly sliced

Clean the fish of any remaining sinew and skin. Slice the fillet into wide, thin pieces about ½-inch thick and season with salt. Arrange the fish in a small container. In a separate bowl, whisk together the garlic, water, vinegar, oregano, paprika, and salt. Pour the mixture over the fish, then cover, shake gently, and place in the refrigerator to marinate for at least 12 hours and up to 2 days.

Heat the peanut oil in a 3- to 4-quart saucepan over medium-high heat until it reaches 375°F on a deep-fry thermometer. Play around with the burner to find the right spot to maintain the oil at 375° with little variation.

Drain the fish and, working in three batches, dredge the fish pieces in the cornmeal, making sure they are evenly coated.

Carefully place the first batch, one at a time, into the hot oil. Cook, undisturbed, until golden brown, 3 to 5 minutes. Remove one piece and cut it open to check for doneness: the fish should flake apart and the breading should adhere to the fish. Remove from the oil and place on a paper towel–lined plate. Repeat until all the fish is cooked.

Transfer the fried fish to a large platter, and serve with aioli, parsley, mint, and chile slices.

MINTED SPICED HERRING WITH FENNEL

SERVES 4

This simple combination is a fun little snack dish. The fennel tones down the vibrant personality of the herring and adds a cool, mellow freshness that pairs nicely with aperitif wines like Albariño or Tocai Friulano. Smoked trout or mackerel make a compelling addition or substitute in this dish. Easy to prepare and make ahead, this is best eaten with toothpicks (and napkins!).

2 small fennel bulbs, cut into thin bite-size slices

Salt

1 (12-ounce) jar herring in wine sauce, drained and 2 tablespoons liquid reserved

Juice of ½ lemon

¼ cup extra-virgin olive oil

1 teaspoon ground mace

2 sprigs mint, leaves torn

Season the fennel lightly with salt and the reserved herring marinade; let sit for a few minutes.

Cut the herring into bite-size pieces and combine with the fennel, along with the lemon juice and olive oil. Refrigerate until ready to serve (up to 1 day).

Just before serving, sprinkle the mace and the torn mint leaves over the dish.

CHILLED OYSTERS
WITH GRILLED MERGUEZ SAUSAGE

MAKES ENOUGH FOR 1 DOZEN OYSTERS

Seasoned with garlic, hot paprika, mint, cumin, and coriander, the lamb sausage known as *merguez* is a traditional Northern African specialty. Swapping bites of this hot sausage with cold oysters is a revelation. This unlikely cultural and culinary pairing was born in Bordeaux, France, where the combination of spicy and briny is a perfect match to the light, fresh styles of red wines produced there.

1 dozen oysters

8 ounces merguez sausage

Plenty of lightly chilled light Bordeaux red wine (optional)

Shuck the oysters and keep very cold until ready to serve. Using either a hot grill or a broiler set to high, cook the *merguez* until the sausage blisters and begins to burst with juices. Remove from the heat and slice into bite-size rounds. To serve, eat a cold briny oyster immediately followed by a bite of hot sausage.

BROILED SCALLOP GRATIN

SERVES 4

There is a great history of seafood dishes coated with various sauces, baked until warmed through, then broiled for a final hit of color and crust. The first step for such recipes is to find a pan that can go from stovetop to broiler and is just large enough for all of the scallops to fit without touching each other. A small sauté pan in combination with a pie pan or baking dish will also suffice. Or, you can broil individual servings in washed scallop shells for a very elegant presentation.

8 large sea scallops

Salt

2 tablespoons butter

½ cup walnuts, crumbled, divided use

1 bulb fennel, very thinly sliced

1 clove garlic, grated

1 teaspoon ground ginger

1 teaspoon mustard powder or Dijon mustard

½ cup white wine

2 tablespoons sour cream or heavy cream

Freshly ground pepper-allspice

Toasted slices of crusty bread

Lightly season the scallops all over with salt. Refrigerate until ready to cook. Preheat the broiler to high.

Melt the butter in a gratin dish or enamel pan over moderate heat. Add ¼ cup of the walnuts, tossing to coat with butter, and cook until fragrant and a shade darker, 3 to 5 minutes. Stir in the fennel and garlic and cook until slightly wilted. Add the ginger and mustard powder, stirring to incorporate. Add the white wine and sour cream and simmer until thickened, about 5 minutes. Season with salt and pepper-allspice. Remove from the heat and nestle the scallops in the warm sauce, spooning the sauce to cover the sides of the scallops but leaving the tops exposed. Scatter the remaining ¼ cup of walnuts over the entire dish.

Place on the top rack of the oven and broil until a light crust has formed and the scallops are lightly colored, crisped, and heated through, about 7 minutes. Serve immediately with crusty bread.

HERB-BAKED CLAMS

SERVES 4 TO 6

Like oysters, clams take well to bold flavors and high heat. This warmly spiced version lets the briny sweet clam shine. A little bit of charring on the crumb mixture is actually desirable, as the bitter smoky flavors complement the dish well. Purposely trying to burn food can be tricky, but who hasn't burned food before? All I'm doing is encouraging you to turn a mistake into a skill. Serve these piping hot, preferably with a very cold rosé wine.

24 cherrystone clams or
12 top neck clams, scrubbed
well under cold running water

1 cup water

3 tablespoons chopped
flat-leaf parsley

1 clove garlic, grated

2 tablespoons fresh lemon juice

2 tablespoons Pernod or
dry vermouth

4 tablespoons butter,
at room temperature

3 tablespoons panko

1 tablespoon mayonnaise

1 teaspoon freshly grated
nutmeg

Preheat the broiler to high. Line an ovenproof tray with rock salt or folded aluminum foil.

Put the clams in a small pot with the water, cover, and steam over high heat until the shells open just a crack, about 7 minutes. Remove the clams from the pot and shuck them, reserving any clam liquor. If using cherrystone clams, arrange half of the shells on the lined tray. If using top neck clams, arrange all of the shells on the tray.

Combine 2 tablespoons of the reserved clam liquor with the parsley, garlic, lemon juice, and Pernod in a small bowl and whisk together. Spoon the herb mixture into the shells and top with the clams. (If using top neck clams, cut the meats in half and place one half in each shell.)

Combine the butter, panko, mayonnaise, and nutmeg in a small bowl and gently work it into a paste. Place a small mound of the butter mixture on top of each clam.

Place the tray on the top rack of the oven and broil until golden brown, 3 to 7 minutes. Remove from the oven and serve immediately.

SAUTÉED CALAMARI
WITH CHILE, HERBS, AND TOMATO

SERVES 4

The texture of calamari takes as well to stewing as it does to frying. And in this dish the calamari is able to infuse the tomato with its rather sultry flavor, while also getting friendly with the chile and herbs. This dish tastes even better if made ahead and refrigerated overnight. To reheat, add a few tablespoons of water and warm gently over low heat. Add the mint just before it hits the table.

3 tablespoons extra-virgin olive oil

1 tablespoon red wine vinegar

2 sprigs thyme, leaves only

1 clove garlic, grated

1½ teaspoons grated fresh ginger

Salt

1½ pounds calamari, cleaned and cut into ½-inch-wide rings

2 tablespoons butter

1 tablespoon crushed red chile flakes

1 (14.5-ounce) can fire-roasted diced tomatoes

2 tablespoons torn mint leaves

Grilled or toasted crusty bread, sliced thick

Combine the olive oil, vinegar, thyme, garlic, ginger, and a good pinch of salt. Add the calamari and toss to combine. Let sit for at least 10 minutes and up to 2 hours.

Heat the butter in a large, heavy sauté pan over high heat. When it begins to bubble, use a slotted spoon to transfer the calamari from the marinade to the pan. Cook, without stirring, 2 to 3 minutes. Add the marinade and the chile flakes, bring to a boil, and cook 2 to 3 minutes more. Stir in the tomatoes and half of a can of water. Reduce the heat to low and simmer until the sauce is reduced and thickened, 10 to 15 minutes. Season with salt and remove from the heat. Add the mint leaves and serve over crusty bread.

SMOKED TROUT PUFFS

SERVES 4

Place a platter of these smoky pastries on the table, along with glasses of iced white vermouth, to help guests settle into the meal. It's one of those dishes that's unexpected yet familiar and very sophisticated. The dough can be made ahead of time and baked straight from the freezer. Easy entertaining, right?

½ cup water

½ cup sour cream or Greek yogurt

8 tablespoons (1 stick) butter

1¼ cups flour

Salt

Freshly ground pepper-allspice

6 eggs

8 ounces smoked trout, skin removed and meat flaked

4 tablespoons finely chopped fresh dill

Bring the water to a boil in a large saucepan. Add the sour cream and butter and simmer until melted. Reduce the heat to low and add the flour. Season with salt and pepper-allspice. Stir vigorously with a wooden spoon until the dough is smooth, slightly elastic, and begins to pull away from the sides of the pan. Remove the pan from the heat and transfer the dough to the bowl of an electric mixer fitted with the paddle attachment (or continue stirring by hand with the wooden spoon).

Add the eggs, one at a time, stirring constantly to make sure each egg is incorporated before adding the next. Don't fret if the dough separates—continued mixing will bring it back together. Gently fold in the trout and dill, taking care not to mash the fish.

Preheat the oven to 400°F. Line a baking sheet with parchment paper.

Using two small spoons, drop tablespoons of dough about 2 inches apart on the lined baking sheet. Bake for 20 minutes and then crack open the oven door and bake until the puffs are golden brown and separate easily from the lined pan, about 5 minutes more. Serve warm.

SHRIMP AL AJILLO

SERVES 4

This dish is ubiquitous in Spain. I ordered it at almost every dive and tapas bar I came across and found it to be universally fantastic. The quantities of oil and booze may seem extravagant, but as this dish vigorously boils into a tasty union, the rich and deliciously flavored sauce becomes as desirable as the shrimp themselves.

⅓ cup olive oil

8 garlic cloves,
very thinly sliced

4 dried árbol or Calabrian
chiles or 2 teaspoons crushed
red chile flakes

2 bay leaves

1¼ pounds medium Gulf
shrimp, peeled and deveined

¾ cup white wine

1 slug brandy (optional)

Juice of ½ lemon

3 tablespoons chopped
flat-leaf parsley

Salt

Crusty bread, for serving

Heat the oil in a large, heavy skillet over high heat. Add the garlic, chiles, and bay leaves, and cook until the garlic begins to color. Carefully add the shrimp and toss to coat with oil, then spread evenly in the pan and cook, without stirring, 3 to 4 minutes. Flip the shrimp, then add the wine and brandy, if using, and bring to a boil. Add the lemon juice and parsley and season generously with salt. Remove from the heat and stir everything together. Serve immediately with plenty of crusty bread.

FRIED SHISITO PEPPERS WITH BOTTARGA

SERVES 4

Bottarga di muggine is the cured and pressed roe of mullet, a specialty of the Mediterranean coast. Though bottarga is often expensive, a small amount will brighten a number of meals, as its flavor blooms incredibly when grated over a warm dish, filling the room with its charismatic salty tang. Any remaining bottarga can be grated over buttered noodles or sliced thinly like carpaccio, topped with sliced celery and drizzled with good-quality olive oil and a little lemon. Crumbled fried seagreens such as dulse or wakame provide a similar umami-rich flavor and can be substituted for the bottarga.

As for the shisitos, there has recently been an incredible increase in availability and interest in small frying peppers that are meant to be eaten whole. The fun of these peppers is that one in every 20 or so is a bully, rudely spicy and not well groomed for polite society. It's a bit of a roulette, since there's no knowing when the fiery kick will get you. It's like accidentally grabbing the single licorice-flavored jelly bean in the Easter basket. But the heat of these peppers is not painful nor does it linger, and soon you'll be diving in for more.

¼ cup peanut oil, divided use

2 pounds fresh shisito or Padrón peppers

1 block bottarga di muggine or bottarga di tonno

1 cup Classic Aioli (page 257)

1 lemon, cut into wedges

Heat 2 tablespoons of the oil in a large, heavy sauté pan over high heat. When the oil is shimmering and hot, add half of the peppers and cook, without stirring, 2 to 3 minutes. Carefully toss the peppers to coat in the oil and cook through until the skins are evenly blistered. Transfer the peppers to a plate lined with paper towels. Quickly repeat the process with the remaining oil and peppers.

When all the peppers have been cooked, transfer them to a serving platter. Using a Microplane® grater, grate some of the bottarga over the peppers. There is no need to salt the peppers, as the bottarga will be plenty enough to season the dish. Grate another 2 tablespoons of the bottarga and stir into the aioli (tightly wrap and refrigerate the remaining bottarga for another use). Serve the peppers with the aioli and lemon wedges on the side.

NEW ORLEANS BBQ SHRIMP

SERVES 4

On a recent trip to New Orleans, I fell hard for these shrimp and ate them at nearly every meal (breakfast included!). Yes, it's incredibly rich, but just as sometimes the party is worth the hangover, these delectable shrimp merit a little butter on your chin. I prefer the 16–20 size shrimp, though larger or smaller are equally good, but I do insist that you use fresh, wild-caught Gulf shrimp. Adjust the cooking time by a few minutes in either direction to accommodate a difference in size.

3 pounds Gulf shrimp, heads and shells on

Salt

1 lemon, halved

12 tablespoons (1½ sticks) butter, divided use

2 tablespoons Creole Seasoning (page 253)

2 cloves garlic, smashed

1 cup white wine

½ cup Worcestershire sauce

2 tablespoons red wine vinegar

2 bay leaves

4 sprigs fresh tarragon

4 tablespoons chopped flat-leaf parsley

Season the shrimp lightly with salt. Heat a large, heavy skillet over high heat until smoking hot, then add the lemon halves, cut sides down, and the shrimp to the dry pan. Cook for 1 minute, then remove all the shrimp and lemon from the pan.

Allow the pan to cool down, then add 8 tablespoons (1 stick) of the butter, the Creole Seasoning, and garlic, and cook over medium heat until the butter is just melted. Add the wine, Worcestershire sauce, vinegar, and bay leaves. Return the shrimp to the pan and bring to a boil. Cook until the shrimp are cooked through, about 5 minutes. Add the remaining 4 tablespoons of butter, tarragon, and chopped parsley and toss to combine. Serve immediately with the lemon halves (and plenty of napkins).

SCALLOP SATAY

SERVES 4

There are few foods so naturally balanced in flavor as scallops, and they pair beautifully with all sorts of seasonings. In this marinade I combine the punch and personality of garlic and ginger, the svelte savor of soy, and peanut butter's hearty richness. This dish is a snap because you do the work once to get the flavor twice, first in the marinade, then in the sauce. For food safety reasons, just make sure that you separate what will become the sauce from what is used to marinate. Round out this dish with Chile-Lime Coleslaw (page 271).

1 pound medium untreated scallops

Salt

2 tablespoons rice vinegar, divided use

2 tablespoons smooth or chunky peanut butter

1 tablespoon soy sauce

1 tablespoon aji-mirin (or substitute maple syrup)

1 clove garlic, grated

1 tablespoon grated fresh ginger

1 tablespoon peanut oil

Season the scallops lightly with salt. Whisk together 1 tablespoon of the vinegar, the peanut butter, soy sauce, mirin, garlic, and ginger. Pour half the marinade over the scallops, tossing gently to combine. Add the remaining 1 tablespoon of vinegar to the unused marinade and whisk to make the sauce; set aside.

Thread 3 to 4 scallops onto a skewer and return to the marinade. Repeat with the remaining scallops. Marinate for at least 20 minutes and up to overnight.

Heat the peanut oil in a large sauté pan over high heat until shimmering. Add the scallop skewers and cook, without moving, until the scallops develop a darkly caramelized crust, about 3 minutes. Turn off the heat and carefully flip the skewers and leave in the pan until cooked through, about 2 minutes.

Drizzle the skewers with the reserved peanut sauce and serve immediately.

CRAWFISH SAUTÉ

SERVES 4

Shrimp are so ubiquitous that it is worth using classic recipes as a stepping stone for trying some of the other wonderful seafoods available. This "crawfish and grits" recipe borrows from that great tradition. I like the way the sour cream balances this fiery combo, offering both richness and cooling relief.

2 cups grits

½ cup sour cream or cream cheese

Salt

4 tablespoons butter, divided use

1 onion, finely diced

2 cloves garlic, sliced

2 teaspoons smoked sweet paprika

1 teaspoon crushed red chile flakes, or to taste

Finely grated zest and juice of 1 lemon

1 pound crayfish meat

1 cup white wine

2 scallions, thinly sliced

Cook the grits according to the package instructions. Once cooked, place a piece of plastic wrap directly on the surface of the grits and keep in a warm place until serving. Before serving, whisk in the sour cream and season with salt.

Heat 2 tablespoons of the butter in a large sauté pan over medium heat. Add the onion and garlic and cook until just wilted, 3 to 4 minutes. Add the paprika, chile flakes, and lemon zest, and cook until toasty and fragrant, about 1 minute.

Add the crayfish meat and any juices. Toss to combine, then add the white wine and lemon juice. Bring the sauce to an energetic simmer and cook until reduced by about half, 4 to 6 minutes. Remove the pan from the heat and whisk in the remaining 2 tablespoons of butter and the scallions.

Spoon the grits into serving dishes and top with the crayfish and their sauce. If you like, serve with lemon wedges and extra chile flakes on the side.

Using Leftover Fish

While cooks are comfortable storing and reheating most other foods, seafood just doesn't seem as appealing the next day. Given seafood's delicate texture and tendency to dry out, the microwave-until-hot technique doesn't cut it. But there are plenty of delicious ways to put those remainders to good use. I like to combine any leftover fish fillets with a few other varieties of seafood and bake them into a potpie, or gently flake the fish and mix it as for a tuna sandwich. That same fish can be lightly dressed and used to garnish a salad of sliced tomatoes and herbs. Or make crisply seared fish cakes. With these options in mind, it might be worth buying and preparing extra seafood just so you can take advantage of the excess to make a quick lunch or snack the next day. As an added win, I've found that kids respond enthusiastically to fish cakes and potpies even if seafood is not typically an easy sell

Reheating Leftover Fish

If left with a good bit of cooked seafood from a previous meal, there is a wonderful way to revive it and turn out a delicious and simple second meal. Place the seafood in a small sauté pan and sprinkle with wine and a few teaspoons of water. Add a couple of cubes of butter and a sprinkle of dried oregano or fresh herbs to give it a lift. Cover the pan with foil and place in a low oven (225°F or so). Let it bake until heated through, 20 to 25 minutes, which will give you plenty of time to make a rice pilaf or some other accompaniment to round out the meal.

WHITE FISH CAKES

SERVES 4

These are as easy to make as crab cakes, and you can use any flaked cooked fish, including canned pink or red salmon, tuna, and even sardines. The trick is to keep the texture of the fish intact, mixing it ever so gently with the bread mixture. Most any herb will do, so take this as an opportunity to use up any sprig stragglers you have in your produce drawer.

1 cup panko

4 tablespoons mayonnaise

2 tablespoons chopped fresh herbs, such as tarragon or parsley

1 tablespoon lemon juice

Salt or Old Bay Seasoning® to taste

1 pound cooked white fish, cooled and flaked

2 tablespoons butter

Combine the panko, mayonnaise, herbs, and lemon juice in a bowl, season with salt, and gently mix together to form a paste. Add the flaked fish and gently mix to combine, taking care not to break up the flakes of fish.

Divide the mixture into four equal cakes, gently forming them into patties slightly taller than they are round. They should be packed just tightly enough so that they will hold together during cooking, but not so hard as to crush the fish.

Preheat the broiler to high.

Heat the butter in a sauté pan over moderate heat until bubbling. Place the cakes in the pan and cook until the edges begin to brown on the bottom. Spoon the butter from the pan over the tops of the cakes and place the whole pan under the broiler and broil until the tops have browned, 5 to 8 minutes.

Remove from the broiler and serve with any sauce you like (see pages 213 to 263 for ideas).

DEVILED CRAB
(OR SCALLOPS OR WHITE FISH)

SERVES 4

As a child of the Chesapeake region, I am pretty partial to blue crab, but this basic recipe is a fun and easy way to serve up any number of seafood varieties. The mixture, "deviled" with a pinch of cayenne, is traditionally baked in the shell of the crab from which the meat was supposedly plucked—a style of entertaining that speaks to an earlier age. I like to use small casserole dishes or cast iron cocottes. Sometimes I even spread the mixture on slices of baguette for a tuna melt–style treat.

6 tablespoons butter

2 teaspoons ground mace

1 large pinch cayenne

1 pound crabmeat, such as blue, red, Dungeness, or Maine, picked

1 tablespoon amontillado sherry

2 tablespoons Dijon mustard

2 tablespoons Worcestershire sauce

3 egg yolks or ¾ cup mayonnaise

2 cups crushed oyster or Ritz® crackers

Toasted slices of baguette

Preheat the oven to 425°F.

Melt the butter in a saucepan over medium heat. Add the mace and cayenne and cook until toasted and fragrant, about 2 minutes. Add the crabmeat and sherry and toss gently to coat. Remove from the heat.

In a separate bowl, whisk together the mustard, Worcestershire sauce, egg yolks, and crushed crackers. Add the crabmeat mixture and mix gently to combine. Spread the crabmeat in a serving dish or crab shells. Bake until the mixture is hot all the way through (this timing will depend on the size of the serving dish).

Preheat the broiler to high and move the crab to the top rack. Broil just until the top is browned. Serve immediately with toasted baguette slices.

FISH TACOS

SERVES 4

Any beautiful ingredients can be combined to make a fish taco, so what follows is not so much a recipe as a series of suggestions. That said, I do have two requirements when I am making tacos: only corn tortillas will do, and sour cream is a must. I think salmon makes the best tacos, as it has an easygoing yet full flavor that can stand its ground next to robust accompaniments. I recommend seasoning the fish with a little dried oregano before cooking and providing fresh cilantro as garnish. I personally adore the aroma of the toasted corn tortilla, the soft texture of the seafood, and the crunch of a cabbage slaw. But the fish taco is ultimately your creation, so throw in some canned black or pinto beans, citrus segments, cucumbers, sliced radishes . . . fish taco is as fish taco does.

1½ pounds seafood, skinned

Light salsa such as tomatillo, or a mild, lightly smoky red salsa

1 cup sour cream

1 avocado, pitted, peeled, and diced

½ bunch cilantro, leaves only

1 recipe Chile-Lime Coleslaw (page 271)

16 corn tortillas

Grill, bake, broil, or poach the seafood, then set aside to cool to room temperature. You may want to marinate the cooked fish in a bit of salsa or a simple vinaigrette. Chilled or precooked seafood is best, as this dish will not stay hot long, and so it is not worth the stress of bringing it all together at an exact moment.

Set out bowls of salsa, sour cream, avocado, cilantro, and coleslaw.

Toast the corn tortillas in a heavy dry pan over medium heat until toasted yet pliable. Keep warm in a kitchen towel. For each taco, stack two tortillas together.

Let everyone build their own tacos just the way they like.

SEAFOOD POTPIE

SERVES
8 AS AN APPETIZER • 4 AS AN ENTREE

Because these flavors are so fresh and light, this potpie works as well for a summery lunch as it does for a wintry supper. The filling can be made ahead of time, and the crust is baked separately and set atop the stew as a garnish. This dish should be served with chilled Beaujolais and a green salad full of fresh herbs and lightly dressed with olive oil and lemon.

FOR THE PASTRY:

2 cups flour, plus extra for rolling

1 tablespoon sugar

2 teaspoons salt

A pinch of cayenne

16 tablespoons (2 sticks) cold butter, cut into cubes

¼ to ½ cup water

FOR THE FILLING:

4 tablespoons butter

5 tablespoons flour

3 cloves garlic, chopped

4 sprigs fresh thyme

2 bay leaves

1 tablespoon onion powder

1 teaspoon ground mace

3 cups milk

6 cups diced vegetables (I suggest 1 cup each of any of the following: diced fennel, diced carrot, diced celery root, quartered small onions, baby potatoes, quartered radish, or diced butternut squash)

2 tablespoons olive oil

Salt

4 pounds mixed seafood, skinned and cut into bite-size pieces (I suggest salmon, haddock, shrimp, and scallops)

1 tablespoon sherry

½ bunch parsley, leaves chopped

1 teaspoon smoked paprika

To make the pastry, whisk together the flour, sugar, salt, and cayenne. Add the cubed butter and toss to coat. Add half of the flour–butter mixture to a food processor and pulse just until it forms large clumps. Remove the processor bowl from the machine and, taking care to avoid the blade, use your hands to squeeze and flatten the clumps. Return the bowl to the machine then add the remaining flour–butter mixture. While pulsing the processor, slowly drizzle in the water just until the dough comes together. Remove from the bowl and form into a loose ball with your hands. Wrap in plastic and refrigerate for 1 hour or up to 2 days.

To make the filling, preheat the oven to 400°F.

Melt the butter in a large saucepan over medium heat. Add the flour and garlic and cook, stirring, just until smooth and pale golden, about 7 minutes. Add the thyme, bay leaf, onion powder, and mace. Whisk in the milk, bring to a simmer, and cook gently over low heat until thickened, 10 to 15 minutes. Remove from the heat and pluck out the thyme and bay leaves. If not using right away, cover the surface of the béchamel with plastic wrap to prevent it from forming a skin.

Meanwhile, toss the vegetables with the olive oil on a large baking sheet and season with salt. Roast until tender, about 15 minutes. Keep the oven on.

Season all the seafood with salt and let rest 5 minutes.

Remove the pastry from the refrigerator and roll it out on a lightly floured work surface until ¼-inch thick. Cut the pastry so that it is roughly the same size as the pot or dish that the potpie will be served in. Transfer the crust to a parchment-lined baking sheet and bake until golden brown, 15 to 20 minutes.

Meanwhile, add the fish and roasted vegetables to the béchamel and stir to combine. Cook over medium heat until the fish is cooked through, about 10 minutes. Remove from the heat and stir in the sherry. Lay the crust over the stew and sprinkle with the chopped parsley and paprika.

OYSTER ROAST

This down and dirty Southern tradition is a great way to get people together to eat far too many oysters, which is a damn good thing. Southern oysters are a must, more so for budgetary reasons than any other. Gather up a bushel and hose them down thoroughly to wash off any mud or grit. Prepare a large wood fire in a fire pit. Traditionally, a thick sheet of metal is placed over the flame, and when it is hot, the oysters are added to steam open in their own juices. You can also use a double thickness of chicken wire, held in place with a few cinderblocks or bricks. Throw down a mess of oysters over the flame. After about a minute, pour a beer or two directly over the oysters, creating an admittedly awesome cloud of steam, which will help the oysters cook quickly and evenly. An alternative method is to throw big sheets of seaweed over the oysters, which will smolder and steam. Hey, you can even do both. The oysters, as they cook, will begin to gape slightly. At this point, remove them all to a table lined heavily with newspaper. Provide every guest with a shucker, or even just an old table knife, as the oysters will yield easily just by inserting a knife into the shells. Serve the oysters straight from the fire with plenty of ice-cold beer, lemon wedges, and a selection of sauces—Tabasco, cocktail, aioli, and, my favorite, rémoulade.

SHRIMP AND PEANUT BOIL

SERVES 6 TO 10

You should probably turn off and put away your phones when this boil is ready to eat. You'll be here for a while—it's a mess of food, and things will get messy!

2 pounds raw peanuts in shell

3 pounds shrimp, shell on

1 cup Creole Seasoning (page 253), divided use

½ cup sea salt

2 (12-ounce) bottles dark beer

2 pounds baby red potatoes

8 ears corn, shucked

1 fresh chile pepper, such as Fresno or serrano

2 pounds smoked sausage, such as andouille or chorizo

3 lemons, cut in quarters

Melted butter, for serving

Hot sauce, for serving

Soak the peanuts in cold water overnight. Marinate the shrimp in ½ cup of the Creole Seasoning for 30 minutes or up to overnight.

The following day, drain the peanuts, then place them in a large stock pot with the sea salt. Add the beer and 1 gallon water. Place a plate over the peanuts to keep them submerged in the liquid, then bring to a simmer. Simmer until the peanuts are soft, about 6 hours, adding more water (or beer) as needed to keep the peanuts covered.

Add the potatoes, corn, and chile and cook until the potatoes are just tender, 10 to 15 minutes. Add the shrimp, sausage, lemons, and the remaining ½ cup of Creole Seasoning, and cook over medium heat for 15 minutes.

Strain off all of the broth then pour all of the boiled goodness onto a large table covered with plenty of newspaper. Serve with bowls of melted butter, hot sauce, and lots of beer.

MUSSELS

The number one reason that I love mussels is that they force you to slow down. It's very hard to be greedy when eating them since each bite must be taken one at a time direct from the shell. This deliciously painstaking process engages us with our food, through touch, taste, aroma, and even through the beautiful architecture created by a growing pile of empty shells. This slowness also allows you to engage with our dinner companions. I can look my wife in the eyes and enjoy her company as we each reach for a mussel and maneuver it to scoop up some of the aromatic broth.

On the flip side of the coin, mussels let you get dinner on the table in a hurry. They are one of the most convenient seafoods. Available in most grocery stores, they are affordable, keep well for a couple days in the fridge, and are super easy to prepare. When buying mussels look for ones that are moist, with no broken or gaping shells. To store them, place them in a casserole dish and cover them with several layers of wet paper towels. Before cooking, rinse them well under cold running water to remove any stowaway grit.

There are few ingredients that don't pair with mussels in one combination or another. It's a great canvas to use up any straggler herbs, those last few stalks of celery, a neglected jar of mustard. You name it, throw it in there. For ideas, take a look at the matrix on pages 65-67, built upon the liquid you will use for steaming. There is no set master recipe, but work from left to right through the matrix as a general guide for when to add ingredients. Play around with combinations, remember your favorites, keep experimenting, slow down, and have fun.

How to Clean Mussels

Put the mussels in a colander and wash under cold running water. Check that all of the mussels are tightly closed. Gently tap any that are open against a hard surface—if they close right away, they are OK to use. If they close lethargically or not at all, discard them. If any mussels have a beard attached, remove it using your thumb and forefinger to grasp and pull it away from the shell. Pat the mussels dry with a towel.

Steamed Mussel Recipe Template

This method works for any quantity of mussels. 2 pounds of mussels make enough for four people as a starter or two as a main course. Serve with lots of crusty bread.

Heat a large, heavy pot over high heat. Add any hearty herbs and spices and toast for 1 minute, then add the mussels. Cook for 1 minute or until the mussels begin to crack open. Add the liquid and any vegetables and/or citrus you have chosen. Cover the pot and cook until the mussels have opened completely, 5 to 7 minutes. Discard any mussels that have not opened. Add all the finishing ingredients and stir to combine. Cover and let sit for 2 minutes, then serve with lots of crusty bread.

LIQUID	HEARTY HERBS	SPICES	VEGETABLES/CITRUS	FINISHING FAT	FINISHING HERBS & GARNISHES
Amber beer	Lemongrass Oregano Thyme	Allspice Bay leaf Cinnamon Coriander	Fennel Fresh chile Fresh ginger Garlic Lemon	Butter	Basil Chives Cilantro Ham Whole grain mustard Tarragon
Bitter-style Belgian beers	Lemongrass Savory Thyme	Allspice Bay leaf Cinnamon Clove Cumin Mace Pepper	Roasted bell pepper Celery Fennel Fresh ginger Roasted garlic Lemon peel Roasted onion Orange peel Roasted shallots Roasted squash	Butter	Chives Cilantro Whole grain mustard Tarragon

LIQUID	HEARTY HERBS	SPICES	VEGETABLES/CITRUS	FINISHING FAT	FINISHING HERBS & GARNISHES
Hoppy beers	Lemongrass Oregano Thyme	Allspice Bay leaf Dried chile Cinnamon stick Cloves Juniper berries Mace Nutmeg Black pepper	Roasted bell pepper Celery Fennel Roasted garlic Ginger Roasted onion Orange peel Roasted shallots	Butter Cream Sour cream	Basil Chive Tarragon
Dark beers	Rosemary Thyme	Allspice Bay leaf Cinnamon stick Ground coriander Juniper berries Mace Pepper	Roasted bell pepper Roasted fennel Roasted garlic Ginger Roasted onion Orange peel Roasted shallots Roasted squash	Butter Nut oils	Chives Cilantro Parsley Tarragon
Stock/water	Lemongrass Savory Thyme	Bay leaf Dried chile Cinnamon stick Ground coriander Mace Pepper Saffron	Roasted bell pepper Chile Chipotle Fennel Garlic Ginger Lemon peel Roasted onion Roasted shallot	Butter Cream Sour cream	Arugula Chive Cilantro Dill Mint Whole grain mustard Parsley Tarragon Diced tomato

LIQUID	HEARTY HERBS	SPICES	VEGETABLES/CITRUS	FINISHING FAT	FINISHING HERBS & GARNISHES
Red wine	Rosemary Savory Thyme	Allspice Bay leaf Cinnamon stick Cloves Juniper berries Mace Nutmeg Pepper	Roasted or fresh fennel Roasted garlic Ginger Lemon peel Roasted onion Orange peel Roasted shallot Roasted squash	Butter Nut oils	Chives Dill Mint Whole grain mustard Parsley Tarragon
White wine	Lemongrass Oregano Savory Thyme	Bay leaf Dried chile Ground coriander Mace Nutmeg Saffron	Roasted bell pepper Chile Chipotle Fennel Garlic Ginger Lemon peel Roasted onion Roasted shallot	Butter Cream Sour cream	Arugula Chive Cilantro Dill Mint Whole grain mustard Parsley Tarragon Diced tomato

PAN-ROASTED MUSSELS OVER APPLEWOOD CHIPS
WITH DRAWN BUTTER

SERVES 4

In addition to the traditional steaming method, I often roast mussels over aromatic components such as wood chips or hardy herbs. This gives them a totally unique flavor and a drier texture, and makes for a very interesting presentation.

2 lemons, halved

1 cup applewood chips

4 pounds mussels, washed in cold water, broken or open shells discarded

¼ cup water

8 tablespoons (1 stick) salted butter

Preheat the oven to 400°F.

Heat a large, heavy pan over high heat. Add the lemons, cut sides down, and the wood chips. Wait a few minutes until the chips begin to smolder and smoke. Before the chips fully ignite, add the mussels to the pan and sprinkle with the water. Quickly cover the pan with aluminum foil and continue to cook over high heat until wisps of smoke begin to seep out of the pan. Transfer the covered pan to the oven and bake until the mussels have opened, 7 to 10 minutes.

Meanwhile, melt the butter and divide it among ramekins. Remove the pan from the oven, set it on the table, and remove the foil, releasing all the rich smoky-briny aromas. Serve immediately with the drawn butter.

PAN-ROASTED MUSSELS OVER BAY LEAVES AND CINNAMON WITH AIOLI

SERVES 4

Your kitchen will smell amazing when you take these mussels from the oven, while the fragrant herbs and spices add just the gentlest whiff of exotic flavor to the mussels.

1 bunch fresh thyme

8 bay leaves, fresh or dried

4 cinnamon sticks

4 star anise pods

4 pounds mussels, washed in cold water and broken or open shells discarded

¼ cup water

Classic Aioli (page 257), melted butter, or fruity olive oil, for serving

Preheat the oven to 400°F.

Heat a large, heavy pan over high heat. Add the thyme, bay leaves, cinnamon, and star anise, and cook for a few minutes until they begin to smolder and smoke. Before the aromatics fully ignite, add the mussels to the pan and sprinkle with the water. Quickly cover the pan with aluminum foil and continue to cook over high heat until wisps of smoke begin to seep out of the pan. Transfer the covered pan to the oven and bake until the mussels have opened, 7 to 10 minutes. Set the pan on the table, remove the foil, and serve immediately with aioli on the side.

SEAFOOD SALADS
AND SANDWICHES

When I'm looking for something to serve away from the comfort of my kitchen, I turn to these recipes. Their emphasis on fresh vegetables and seafood served chilled or at room temperature, not to mention their one-plate, grab-and-go convenience, make these perfect picnic meals. The only downside of traveling with all these ingredients is that it can require a lot of Tupperware®, but that's a small price to pay for the ease of a delicious meal that can be enjoyed anywhere.

SHRIMP AND ARUGULA SALAD WITH HORSERADISH-LEMON DRESSING

SERVES 4

After a trip to Leon's Oyster Shop in Charleston, South Carolina, my wife could not stop talking about this dish, and we immediately tried to re-create it. The generous use of horseradish was clearly the salad's hook, its racy kick placed front and center. While horseradish is commonly prepared with vinegar, we chose to soften its character with the sweeter, gentler acid of lemon juice. The remaining components of the salad—sweet shrimp, peppery arugula, and cool parsley—was a fine example of the chef's restraint.

Make sure to use the freshest Gulf shrimp you can find, as there is little for lesser-quality product to hide behind. I highly recommend you buy raw, shell-on shrimp to poach them yourself and peel and dress them while they are still warm.

1¼ pounds cooked shrimp, peeled (see page 186 for instructions on deep poaching)

4 tablespoons mayonnaise

4 teaspoons prepared horseradish

Juice of 1½ lemons, divided use

A pinch of cayenne

Salt

1 pound arugula

1 bunch parsley, leaves only

1 tablespoon olive oil

Combine the shrimp with the mayonnaise, horseradish, juice of 1 lemon, and cayenne. Season with salt and gently mix together. Let sit for at least 15 minutes.

Combine the arugula and parsley in a large bowl and toss with the olive oil, remaining lemon juice, and salt to taste. Garnish with the dressed shrimp and serve immediately.

KING CRAB COBB SALAD

SERVES 4

The original Cobb was essentially a garden salad that was billed as a main dish. It included a bounty of novel ingredients that suddenly could be shipped by freight from far-flung agricultural areas. There were so many new and delicious tastes all together on one plate. Imagine how cool such a composition must have been at the time! I include a recipe here because bringing together so many great tastes and textures is still a cool thing—not to mention pretty damn delicious.

2 large ripe tomatoes, cored and diced

Salt

Double recipe of Red Wine Vinaigrette (page 81), divided use

2 heads Belgian endive or 1 head chicory, chopped

1 bunch watercress, trimmed

2 avocados, pitted, peeled, and thinly sliced

2 pounds king crab legs, shelled and cut into ½-inch pieces

4 hard-boiled eggs, sliced

1 lemon, quartered

Freshly ground pepper-allspice

Season the tomatoes with salt and toss with half of the vinaigrette. Let marinate for 10 minutes.

Divide the endive, watercress, avocados, crabmeat, hard-boiled eggs, and lemon equally among 4 plates. Drizzle the remaining vinaigrette over the salads and season with salt. Divide the marinated tomatoes among the salads and season with freshly ground pepper-allspice.

UPDATED CRAB LOUIS

SERVES 4

This salad is a classic for a reason—it comes together in minutes and tastes phenomenal.

1 cup plain Greek yogurt

½ cup mayonnaise

4 tablespoons chili sauce or ketchup

3 tablespoons Worcestershire sauce

Juice of 2 lemons, divided use

1 tablespoon garlic powder

2 teaspoons onion powder

Tabasco, to taste

Salt

2 pounds crabmeat, picked

2 pounds asparagus, trimmed and briefly blanched in salted water

2 heads endive, trimmed and leaves separated

8 large radishes, very thinly sliced

4 ounces spicy salad greens or arugula

In a small bowl, whisk together the yogurt, mayonnaise, chili sauce, Worcestershire sauce, half of the lemon juice, garlic powder, onion powder, and Tabasco to taste. Taste for seasoning and adjust with salt and Tabasco as desired.

In a separate bowl, gently toss the crabmeat with the remaining lemon juice.

Spoon a dollop of the sauce onto each of four plates and, using the back of the spoon, spread it into a circle. Arrange the asparagus, endive, radishes, and greens over the sauce. Scatter the dressed crab over the vegetables and finish with a dollop of sauce.

CAESAR SALAD

SERVES 4

The Caesar salad has unfortunately become one of those culinary sacred cows—chefs don't like making it, few diners order it, but riots would ensue if it were removed from menus. I don't want to see the Caesar vanish, but neither do I want to see it languish. So I refreshed this old standby by positioning the briny savor of anchovies front and center and replacing bland romaine with the bitter crunch of chicory.

9 eggs, hard-boiled and peeled

6 tablespoons extra-virgin olive oil

3 tablespoons red wine vinegar

3 tablespoons whole grain mustard

3 (2-ounce) cans anchovy fillets in olive oil, drained (oil reserved) and chopped

Salt

2 heads chicory or 1 pound baby kale leaves

8 slices rustic bread

2 cloves garlic, halved

Freshly ground pepper-allspice

Mash 1 egg with the olive oil, vinegar, mustard, and anchovy oil. Stir in the chopped anchovies. Taste the dressing and season lightly with salt if desired. (It won't need much, if any.)

Discard the tough outer leaves from the chicory. Tear the tender inner leaves into 1-inch pieces and transfer to a salad bowl. Toss the chicory with the dressing until evenly coated. Divide the salad among four plates. Slice the remaining eggs into thin rounds and divide them among the plates.

Toast the bread and, while still hot, lightly rub the cut side of the garlic cloves on the toast. Season the salads with freshly cracked pepper-allspice and serve with the toasts.

BOTTARGA AND ENDIVE SALAD

SERVES 4

This is a very elegant first course salad that can be embellished as you like with roasted parsnips, crushed walnuts, golden raisins, or thin slices of Granny Smith apple. If you do include any (or all!) of these suggestions, you will need to tinker with the amount of vinaigrette to ensure you have the right balance. For more information on bottarga, see page 46.

1 (¼-inch-thick) slice fresh ginger

Juice of ½ lemon

4 tablespoons walnut, almond, or mild extra-virgin olive oil

Salt

2 heads Belgian endive, trimmed

2 bunches watercress, trimmed

2 cups chervil leaves or flat-leaf parsley (with stems cut into bite-size pieces)

1 to 2 ounces bottarga

Freshly ground pepper-allspice (optional)

Rub the ginger against the sides of a large mixing bowl to perfume the bowl; discard the ginger. Add the lemon juice, oil, and a small amount of salt. Add the endive, watercress, and chervil, and toss gently to combine. Divide the salad among four plates.

Using a Microplane grater, grate the bottarga over each salad. Garnish with freshly ground pepper-allspice, if desired.

TOMATO SALAD WITH POACHED HALIBUT

SERVES 2

The sweet-cool combo of tomato, parsley, and mint brings out the very best in mild halibut. The fish's poaching liquid is reduced and used as the salad's vinaigrette.

1 pound halibut fillet, skinned

Salt

⅓ cup extra-virgin olive oil

¼ cup red wine vinegar

2 tablespoons Pernod

1 shallot, thinly sliced and briefly rinsed under cold water

2 large ripe tomatoes, preferably a mix of heirloom varieties, cored and cut in thin wedges (or quartered for smaller ones)

2 cups flat-leaf parsley leaves, torn

1 cup mint leaves, torn

Freshly ground pepper-allspice (optional)

Season the fish with salt and place it in a shallow sauté pan that is just slightly larger than the halibut. Add the olive oil, vinegar, Pernod, shallot, and enough water to come halfway up the sides of the fish. Place the pan over very low heat and let it slowly come to a simmer, 7 to 10 minutes. Gently flip the fish and cook 5 minutes more. Remove the fish from the pan and transfer to a plate to cool.

Meanwhile, bring the cooking liquid to a boil over medium-high heat and boil until reduced to about ½ cup. Remove from the heat and refrigerate until cooled.

Combine the tomatoes, parsley, mint, and chilled cooking liquid in a large bowl, tossing gently to coat. Taste for seasoning and adjust if necessary. Arrange the salad on a large platter and gently flake the cooled halibut over the salad. Garnish with freshly ground pepper–allspice, if desired.

KELP SALAD
WITH ORANGE AND FENNEL

SERVES 4

Orange and fennel are a classic combination. Fold in the salty tang of kelp, smoothed by a jot of sesame, and this salad becomes a wonderful way to introduce seagreens into your diet. The vegetables taste best shaved razor-thin on an adjustable blade slicer.

1 pound fresh or frozen kelp (or 2 ounces dried kelp, rehydrated and drained), torn into bite-size pieces

3 oranges, peeled and cut into segments

1 large fennel bulb, very thinly sliced

1 Vidalia onion, very thinly sliced

4 radishes, very thinly sliced

1 tablespoon sherry vinegar

2 tablespoons sesame oil

Salt

Combine the kelp, oranges, fennel, onion, radishes, vinegar and sesame oil in a large bowl. Season with salt and toss gently to combine. Let sit for 10 minutes before serving.

DILLED POTATO SALAD
WITH SMOKED TROUT

SERVES 4

This potato salad keeps its interest through to the last bite, thanks to its luxurious sour cream dressing spiked with plenty of vinegar, all balanced by smoky flakes of fish. Given its richness, this is best served as an appetizer.

1 pound fingerling potatoes

6 ounces smoked trout, skin removed and reserved

2 cloves garlic

Salt

4 tablespoons sour cream

4 tablespoons red wine vinegar

1 bunch dill, chopped (save a few fronds for garnish)

1 head radicchio or endive, leaves separated

Combine the potatoes, trout skin, garlic, and a generous amount of salt in a small pot and cover with cold water. Bring to a boil and cook until the potatoes are tender but not falling apart, about 10 minutes. Drain the potatoes, reserving the garlic. Discard the trout skin.

Whisk together the sour cream, vinegar, chopped dill, and boiled garlic in a large bowl, mashing the garlic to incorporate it into the dressing. While the potatoes are still warm, add them to the dressing and gently stir until fully incorporated. Arrange the radicchio leaves on a platter and spoon the potato salad over top. Using your hands, break the trout fillet into small flakes and scatter over the salad. Garnish with the remaining dill fronds.

SALADE NIÇOISE
WITH RED WINE VINAIGRETTE

SERVES 4

This classic Provençal dish combines a diversity of flavors and textures into a lovely, out of the ordinary, and wholly satisfying meal. Take some time to enjoy a lingering lunch with a glass of rosé, as they do in France.

FOR THE RED WINE VINAIGRETTE:

4 tablespoons whole grain mustard

4 tablespoons red wine vinegar

1 clove garlic, grated

⅓ cup extra-virgin olive oil

2 (5-ounce) cans oil-packed U.S. albacore tuna or Alaska sockeye or pink salmon, drained and oil reserved

Salt

FOR THE SALAD:

¾ pound new potatoes

2 strips orange peel

Salt

1 pound green beans, trimmed

3 bunches watercress, trimmed

1 head radicchio

2 large tomatoes, cored and cut into wedges

4 radishes, very thinly sliced

1 small red onion, thinly sliced and rinsed briefly under cold water

4 hard-boiled eggs, quartered

½ cup pitted olives, preferably Niçoise

4 sprigs fresh basil, leaves only, gently torn

Freshly ground pepper-allspice

To make the vinaigrette, whisk together the mustard, vinegar, and grated garlic in a small bowl. While whisking, slowly add the olive oil and reserved tuna oil. Season to taste with salt. Set aside.

To make the salad, place the potatoes in a pan just large enough to hold them. Add the orange peel and a generous amount of salt, and cover with cold water. Bring to a boil and cook until the potatoes are easily pierced with a knife, about 10 minutes.

Meanwhile, place the green beans in a colander and set in the sink. Slowly drain the potatoes over the green beans, allowing the hot water to very lightly blanch the beans. Discard the orange peel.

Slice the potatoes into thin rounds and gently toss with one-third of the vinaigrette. Arrange the potatoes, green beans, watercress, and radicchio on a very large platter or on four individual plates. Layer the tomatoes, radishes, onions, and eggs around the platter.

Gently flake the tuna and scatter it evenly over the dish. Garnish the dish with the olives and basil, then drizzle over the remaining vinaigrette. Offer freshly ground pepper-allspice on the side.

ROASTED PEPPER AND
SWEET POTATO SALAD WITH TUNA

SERVES 4

This dish, inspired by my time in Spain, combines super nutritious foods in a very beautiful way. It also works well packed into Tupperware for a convenient lunch on the go. As this salad's flavor improves over time, make a large batch of it ahead of a busy week or even in advance of a dinner party.

2 red bell peppers

1 pound fingerling potatoes

½ pound sweet potato, cut into 1-inch pieces

Salt

2 (5-ounce) cans water-packed U.S. albacore tuna, water drained and reserved

6 ounces slivered almonds, toasted

3 tablespoons Classic Aioli (page 257) or mayonnaise

2 tablespoons extra-virgin olive oil

1 teaspoon freshly grated nutmeg, for garnish

Roast the peppers directly over the burners of a gas stove or under the broiler until the skins are blackened all over. Remove from the heat and place in a loosely sealed bag to steam. Taking care to save any juices, peel the peppers (it's okay to leave some black flecks or small patches of skin). Remove and discard the seeds, then cut the peppers into thin strips.

Meanwhile, place the fingerlings and sweet potatoes in a pan with a generous pinch of salt and the reserved tuna water, cover with cold water, and cook until they can be easily pierced with a knife, about 10 minutes. Drain the potatoes, then toss gently with the almonds, aioli, reserved pepper juices, and olive oil to combine.

Arrange the potato mixture on a platter and top with the pepper strips and any juices. Gently flake the tuna and scatter it over the salad. Sprinkle the nutmeg over the salad and serve.

WALDORF SALAD WITH
SMOKED BLUEFISH, APPLE, AND FENNEL

SERVES 4

Bluefish is, simply put, my favorite fish in the sea. When smoked, it retains a velvety texture, which contrasts nicely with this salad's crisp fennel, celery, and apple. Smoked salmon, sablefish, mackerel, or other hot smoked seafood make great substitutes should bluefish not be available. This salad is best served as a first course, as its flavors are intense and a little goes a long way. If possible, use an adjustable blade slicer to cut the vegetables and apple razor-thin.

5 stalks celery, very thinly sliced

2 large fennel bulbs, very thinly sliced, fronds reserved

1 crisp apple, such as Fuji or Gala, very thinly sliced

1½ cups walnut pieces, toasted

4 tablespoons walnut or extra-virgin olive oil

2 tablespoons fresh orange juice

2 tablespoons sherry vinegar

Salt

1 pound smoked bluefish, skinned and flaked

Combine the celery, fennel, apples, and walnuts in a large bowl. Add the walnut oil, orange juice, and vinegar. Toss to combine, making sure to separate the apple slices, as they can stick together. Season lightly with salt (the bluefish will further season the dish). Divide the salad among four plates and garnish with the flaked fish.

SAIGON FISH SANDWICH

MAKES 4 SANDWICHES

This sandwich, a new spin on a classic *banh mi*, is best built around a full-flavored fish such as mackerel. Grilling the fish produces a pleasantly bitter, smoky char that adds a depth and richness that is perfectly counterbalanced by the pickled veg and cool herbs. In a departure from tradition, butter-toasting the baguette adds great texture and helps brings these flavors into focus.

1 large carrot, julienned

1 small red onion, very thinly sliced and rinsed briefly under cold water

3 tablespoons rice wine vinegar

1 tablespoon aji-mirin or 2 teaspoons sugar

1 to 1½ pounds fillets of mackerel, pompano, bluefish, or other dense fish

Salt

1 large baguette, cut into four 6-inch lengths

2 tablespoons butter

½ bunch cilantro, leaves only

4 sprigs basil, leaves torn

Combine the carrots and onions in a small bowl. Combine the vinegar and mirin in a small saucepan and bring to a boil. Pour the hot vinegar mixture over the carrots and onions and let sit for 10 minutes.

Meanwhile, season the fish with salt and grill, bake, or broil the fillets on high heat, turning once, until cooked through, 5 to 10 minutes, depending on the thickness of the fillets. Remove from the heat.

Slice open the lengths of baguette without cutting all the way through. Heat the butter in a large sauté pan over medium heat. Gently open up the bread and arrange in the pan, facedown, and toast until crisp and golden-brown. Remove the bread from the pan and lay open on a work surface. Place the fish, either hot or chilled, on the bread. Add the pickled carrots and onions, top with the cilantro and basil, and serve.

SMOKED MACKEREL, LETTUCE, AND TOMATO SANDWICH

SERVES 1

The way some people love bacon is the way we fish folk feel about smoked fish. I call for a hot-smoked mackerel for this sandwich; its gentle snap and taut texture are needed for contrast against the juicy tomato. To complete this combination, only a bitter, rugged lettuce, such as frisée or radicchio, will do. This is meant to be a big, filling sandwich, so don't be shy about piling on the goods.

Bread of your choice (I prefer a 6-inch length of baguette, sliced lengthwise)

1 tablespoon mayonnaise

1 tablespoon prepared horseradish

½ fillet smoked mackerel (or any other hot-smoked fish, such as salmon or trout), skinned and flaked into thumb-size pieces

5 to 6 leaves frisée or radicchio

1 medium tomato, sliced thin

Salt

Toast the bread until golden brown. Spread one side with mayonnaise, the other with horseradish. Arrange the smoked fish, frisée, and tomato slices over one side of the bread. Season the tomato with salt. Close the sandwich and serve, with any remaining tomato slices on the side.

THE PO' BOY

The key to a good po' boy is a good bun. I recommend a not-too-crusty French bread that's been toasted in a bit of butter. Layer in a heap of coleslaw topped by about 6 ounces of fried seafood per person. (The Chile-Lime Coleslaw, page 271, is my favorite, but most any slaw will do.) Garnish the sandwich with any sauce you like, though a mayo-based sauce like rémoulade is traditional.

This classic Southern sandwich is usually a vehicle for more neutrally flavored seafood, such as sweet shrimp, Gulf oysters, or white fish such as catfish or flounder. I always prefer a richer fish, and my first choice is mackerel. But because there are so many delicious ways to make a po' boy, I'm not including a definitive recipe, just some suggestions for filling combinations. The green goddess dressing and cool watercress make a particularly nice foil to the fish's crisp coating.

Different creative combinations for Po' Boys (See page 192 for tips on frying fish.)

- Mackerel with Green Goddess Dressing (page 263)

- Fried Oyster with Louisiana Rémoulade (page 215)

- Fried Clam with NOLA Rémoulade (page 216)

- Fried Flounder or Catfish with Fresh Tomato Salsa (page 248) or Spicy Marinara Sauce (page 247)

- Fried Shrimp with Pesto (any of the three on page 261)

FISH STOCKS, SOUPS, AND STEWS

Fish soups and stews can run the gamut from light, acidic, and refreshing to deeply rich, flattered with additions of cream or bacon. Fish soups and stews should be delicious, unfussy, and simple to prepare. The first (and basically only) rule is this: Buy great-quality seafood.

One of the drawbacks of seafood cookery is that it rarely offers an opportunity for the sort of slow flavor development that you get from traditional meat cookery, such as when braising. Most chefs I know show great pride in these preparations as they allow for subtle flavors to be coaxed into incredibly balanced and complex dishes. Most fish soups and stews descend not from chefs but from fishermen. These simple, one-pot dishes are generally an artifact of everyday meals cooked on board or on shore by fishermen, using whatever they were able to catch. These workingman meals reflect the coastal regions and villages from which their boats sailed. Over time, these soups and stews have found their way on to more elegant tables. Not only has our modern cookery adapted these traditions, so has our language. *Chaudière*, the French term for the cast iron pot in which these meals were simmered, has evolved, over time, to now name a dish we well know: chowder.

The foundation of these archetypal stews was rarely more than water. Today, we augment them with robust stocks, enrich them with cream, and fortify them with brandy. While these garnishes add personality, it is important that each type of seafood should remain distinct while working in concert with the other flavors.

This selection of soups and stews represent just a few examples, many European, of how fish and regional ingredients are combined. While there is plenty of debate, at times heated, regarding the specifics and provenance of a certain stew, the recipes below do not claim any authority in such matters. By all means, borrow a component of one to use in another or just generally read through to get a feel for the process. Then go make up your own (that's how I like to work!). For the most part, these recipes are easy to make and prove a wonderful opportunity to utilize whatever your fishmonger hands over when you say, "Give me what's best."

Fish Stocks

Fish cooks very quickly, which means that broths or accompaniments have little time to integrate with that delicious seafood flavor. This is where a seafood stock comes in. The addition of stock can add desired complexity while highlighting the personality of the seafood in the dish. Stock is also essential for any of the traditional stews and classic shore-side dishes such as paella, bouillabaisse, and bisques.

The best stocks are made with super-fresh bones and trimmings and the best aromatic vegetables simmered gently under a watchful eye. Such effort yields an elixir that is at once complementary in flavor and inconspicuous in its presence, with a wonderfully fresh personality.

Fish stock, or *fumet*, is most often made from delicately flavored white fish such as halibut, flounder, or other ground fish. Highly flavored fish, such as snapper, black bass, or grouper, will yield a much richer, weighty stock that is rarely used due to its robust flavor. Gelatinous cartilage or bones from fish such as monkfish or sturgeon require slightly longer periods of extraction and produce a velvety, richly textured stock with a pronounced meaty flavor. Steer clear of very robust species such as mackerel and bluefish, as their oiliness can overwhelm the intended dish.

In a pinch, you can make a very quick fish stock by simmering store-bought low-sodium vegetable stock with a pound of mussels or seafood trimmings, commonly available at seafood counters. It's not the cheapest or most elegant stock, but it's certainly more flavorful than water.

Shellfish stocks, made by searing the shells in oil, then simmering them in wine and water, also have many applications. If a dish needs a spike of briny sea flavor and you don't have any stock on hand, using bottled clam juice is a great quick fix.

BASIC FISH STOCK

MAKES ABOUT 3 QUARTS

A few things to keep in mind when making this stock: Try not to move the pot at all during cooking, which will produce a stock with the cleanest flavor and clarity. Use a good-quality wines and wine vinegar. Always go light with the celery (you can always add more to the dish later, but can't remove its flavor). This stock is best used for dishes such as bouillabaisse that call for adding lots of seafood, layering in additional flavor. It's also great when used as the base for clear broth soups such as *pho*.

4 tablespoons butter

2 pounds fish bones and/or trimmings from mild-flavored fish, such as black bass, flounder, and/or halibut

2 cups sliced fennel with fronds

1 stalk celery, sliced

2 cups white wine

1 cup red or white wine vinegar

10 allspice berries or 5 juniper berries

5 peppercorns

1½ teaspoons salt

3 quarts water

Heat the butter in a large, wide pot (8 quarts or bigger) over medium-low heat. Add the fish bones and/or trimmings and cook, without stirring, until they are almost cooked through, about 15 minutes.

Add the fennel, celery, wine, vinegar, allspice, peppercorns, and salt. Cook until the liquid begins to steam and the alcohol dissipates, about 5 minutes. Add the water and bring to a gentle simmer. Simmer for 20 minutes then turn off the heat. Let the stock sit for 10 minutes, allowing the solids to settle.

Ladle the liquid off and pour through a strainer into a bowl. Once you reach the bottom of the pot, pour the remaining liquid through a strainer into a separate bowl. Let it sit for a few minutes to allow the particles to settle. Ladle off the clear liquid from the top, discarding any liquid that is murky. Discard all the solids and combine the two stocks. Use immediately, refrigerate, or freeze for later use. This stock can be refrigerated for 2 to 3 days or frozen for up to 3 months. (When the stock chills, it will have a loose, gelatinous texture.)

HADDOCK BONE STOCK

MAKES ABOUT 3 QUARTS

Haddock has more briny tang than the sweeter fish I recommend in the Basic Fish Stock recipe (page 93). I like both styles equally, but use them differently. Haddock stock is best for hearty, robust dishes like thick stews or fish chowders.

4 tablespoons butter

3 pounds haddock, cod, or pollock carcasses, gills and discolored spots removed

2 cups white wine

2 celery stalks, cut into large pieces

1 leek, green part only, chopped

½ onion, sliced

1 sprig fresh marjoram or thyme

1 tablespoon fennel seeds

1 pod star anise

1½ teaspoons salt

3 quarts water

Heat the butter in a large, wide pot (8 quarts or bigger) over medium-low heat. Add the fish carcasses and cook, without stirring, until they are almost cooked through, about 15 minutes.

Add the wine, celery, leek, onion, marjoram, fennel seeds, star anise, and salt. Reduce the heat to low and cook until the liquid begins to steam and the alcohol dissipates, about 5 minutes. Add the water and bring to a gentle simmer. Simmer for 20 minutes, and then turn off the heat. Let the stock sit for 10 minutes, allowing the solids to settle.

Ladle the liquid off and pour through a strainer into a bowl. Once you reach the bottom of the pot, pour the remaining liquid through a strainer into a separate bowl. Let it sit for a few minutes to allow the particles to settle. Ladle off the clear liquid from the top, discarding any liquid that is murky. Discard all the solids and combine the two stocks. Use immediately or refrigerate or freeze for later use. This stock can be refrigerated for 2 to 3 days or frozen for up to 3 months. (When the stock chills, it will have a loose, gelatinous texture.)

SEAGREEN STOCK

MAKES ABOUT 3 QUARTS

While it does not have the sweet sea brine flavor of a fumet, seagreen broth can be used almost anywhere a fish, chicken, or vegetable stock is called for, imparting umami and a gently briny aroma to soups, sauces, and braises. Use this broth as is, or season it with lemon and herbs and serve as a consommé. Try adding mace, dried or fresh chile, onion, fennel, or fennel seeds for greater depth of flavor. This broth should be light, sharp, and clear in flavor. Take care not to boil it—excessive cooking will make it lose its focus. For more information on seagreens, see page 139.

1 cup white wine

2 strips lemon zest

2 slices fresh ginger

2 pods star anise

3 quarts water

2 ounces dried kelp

½ cup bonito flakes

Combine the wine, lemon zest, ginger, and star anise in a 6-quart pot over medium heat and simmer until the alcohol dissipates, about 5 minutes. Add the water and bring to a simmer. Add the kelp, bring to a gentle simmer, and cook for 15 minutes.

Using a slotted spoon, remove the seagreens and reserve for another use. Add the bonito flakes, remove from the heat, and let steep for 10 minutes. Strain, discarding all solids. Refrigerate for up to 4 days, or freeze up to 1 month.

SHELLFISH STOCK

MAKES ABOUT 3 QUARTS

A rich shellfish stock can bring incredible depth and complexity to many dishes and is absolutely essential as the base for a shellfish bisque. But because its flavor is so unique, shellfish stock is likely to compete with (if not overpower) more subtle flavors such as delicate white fish, sauces, and soups. This recipe can be made from either lobster or shrimp, or a combination. Keep an eye out for fresh Gulf shrimp at your local market, and request those with shells and heads on. The simple labor of peeling these at home is well worth the bounty of flavorful shells. Lobster bodies (the head and discarded claw and tail shells) are commonly available from most grocery stores that steam lobsters for you.

4 tablespoons butter

4 tablespoons vegetable oil

6 lobster bodies or 3 cups shrimp heads/shells

1 onion, chopped

1 leek, green part only, sliced

3 carrots, chopped

2 stalks celery, chopped

2 bay leaves

1 pod star anise

3 cups white wine

4 tablespoons brandy

Salt

3 quarts water

Heat the butter and vegetable oil in a large, wide stock pot over high heat. Add the lobster bodies and cook until colored all over, about 10 minutes. Using tongs, remove the bodies and reserve. Add the onion, leek, carrots, celery, bay leaves, and star anise and cook over medium-high heat, stirring occasionally, until they just begin to wilt, about 5 minutes. Return the lobster bodies to the pot. Add the wine and brandy. Bring to a boil, and cook until the alcohol smell dissipates, about 5 minutes. Season generously with salt. Reduce the heat to low, add the water, and bring to a simmer. Cook, covered, for 1 hour.

Remove from the heat and let the stock sit for 10 minutes, allowing the solids to settle.

Ladle the liquid off and pour through a strainer into a bowl. Once you reach the bottom of the pot, pour the remaining liquid through a strainer into a separate bowl. Let sit for a few minutes to let the particles settle. Ladle off the clear liquid from the top, discarding any liquid that is murky. Discard all the solids and combine the two stocks. Use immediately or refrigerate or freeze for later use. This stock can be refrigerated for 2 to 3 days or frozen for up to 3 months. (When the stock chills, it will have a loose, gelatinous texture.)

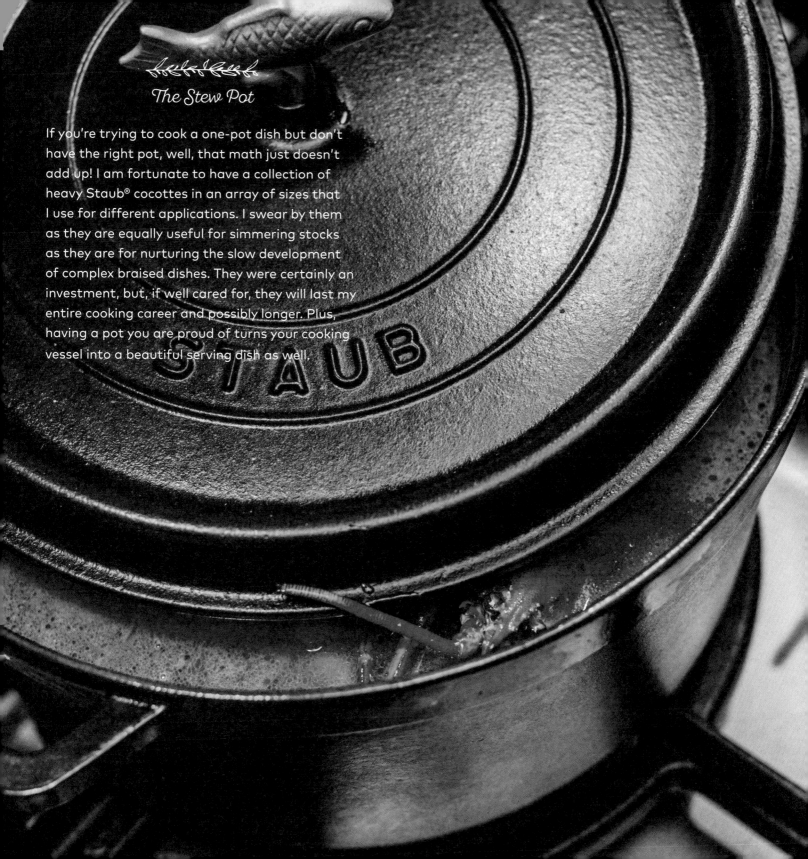

The Stew Pot

If you're trying to cook a one-pot dish but don't have the right pot, well, that math just doesn't add up! I am fortunate to have a collection of heavy Staub® cocottes in an array of sizes that I use for different applications. I swear by them as they are equally useful for simmering stocks as they are for nurturing the slow development of complex braised dishes. They were certainly an investment, but, if well cared for, they will last my entire cooking career and possibly longer. Plus, having a pot you are proud of turns your cooking vessel into a beautiful serving dish as well.

Soups

SMOKED HADDOCK CHOWDER

SERVES 4

Silken flakes of the classic Scottish specialty Finnan Haddie (page 210), a brined and slow smoked haddock, are a perfect addition to creamy chowder. I call for a lot of potato in this recipe, as I prefer my chowders to be overflowing with ingredients—a full meal in themselves. This tastes best if made ahead, refrigerated, and then very gently reheated.

3 tablespoons butter, plus more for garnish, if desired

1 onion, finely diced

1 large fennel bulb, finely diced

2 sprigs fresh thyme

½ cup white wine

2 cups water

1½ pounds red or gold potatoes, cut into ½-inch dice

1 bay leaf

Salt

1 to 1½ pounds Finnan Haddie (page 210)

3 cups milk

1 cup heavy cream

Paprika, for garnish

Heat the butter in a large pan over medium heat. Add the onion and fennel and cook until they begin to glisten, about 2 minutes. Add the thyme and white wine and bring to a boil. Add the water, potatoes, and bay leaf and season with salt. Bring to a boil and cook for 2 minutes. Nestle the Finnan Haddie fillets neatly in the potatoes, then add the milk and cream and bring to a low simmer. Cover the pot and simmer gently until the potatoes are fully cooked and the fish has been poached through, 20 to 25 minutes. Remove from the heat and, using a spatula, gently remove the fish. Peel off the skin and discard. Let the fish sit until cool enough to handle. Using your hands, flake the fish into just-smaller-than-bite size pieces and return them to the chowder.

Let the chowder sit for at least 1 hour and preferably refridgerate for a day before gently reheating and serving. Garnish each bowl with a small pat of butter and a light sprinkle of paprika, if desired.

OYSTER STEW

SERVES 2

My favorite place to eat this stew is the Grand Central Oyster Bar in New York City, where one man watches over a station of miniature steam kettles and churns out hundreds of orders a night. I don't recommend making this for more than two people in one pot, as it becomes hard to manage the heat; I tend to overcook the oysters as I'm sloshing around, searching for them in the liquid. If you want to serve 4, simply set up two pots next to each other on the stove and increase the ingredients proportionally. This dish can be adapted to include almost any shellfish or pristinely fresh fish.

1 clove garlic, halved

2½ cups whole milk

12 large oysters, shucked, liquor reserved

2 tablespoons butter

Dash of amontillado sherry

Salt

Smoked sweet paprika or freshly ground pepper-allspice

Lots of crusty bread or oyster crackers

Rub the garlic clove inside a medium saucepan in order to give soup just a scent of garlic. Discard the garlic, add the milk, and bring to steaming over low heat. Add the shucked oysters and their liquor and simmer until the edges of the oysters begin to curl, 5 to 7 minutes. Add the butter and sherry and season with salt. When the butter has melted, divide the stew into 2 bowls. Garnish with either paprika or pepper-allspice, and serve immediately with bread or crackers.

CALDO VERDE WITH SEAGREENS

SERVES 4 TO 8

Is kelp the new kale? This spin on the great Portuguese potato and kale stew, in which I replace the traditional greens with seagreens, might just convince you. Adding the traditional linguiça sausage and smoked mussels will make this hearty veggie-centric stew even more substantial. Its warm, rustic flavors make it especially welcome after a long day's labor, but it's equally delicious eaten cold, so a big batch made at the beginning of the week can provide a number of convenient on-the-run meals.

5 tablespoons olive oil, divided use

1 onion, finely chopped

2 cloves garlic, finely chopped

6 russet potatoes, peeled and chopped into 1 inch pieces

3 quarts Seagreen Stock (page 95) or water (if making a seagreen stock for this dish use dried kelp and reserve it for use in the soup)

Salt

1 pound fresh or frozen kelp, chopped, or 2 ounces dried kelp (see page 279)

1 pound linguiça sausage, cut into ½-inch rounds (optional)

6 ounces smoked mussels, either canned or fresh packed (optional)

Freshly ground black pepper to garnish

Heat 3 tablespoons of the olive oil in a large saucepan over medium heat. Add the onion and garlic and cook for 3 minutes. Add the potatoes and cook about 5 minutes. Add the stock, season with salt, and bring to a boil. Reduce the heat and simmer until the potatoes begin to fall apart, about 20 minutes. Gently mash the potatoes with a spoon or potato masher until you have a thick, chunky porridge. Stir in the seagreens, cover, and simmer until the greens are tender and deep green, about 15 minutes. If using dried kelp, remove the leaves, chop them into small pieces, and return them to the soup. Add the sausage and/or mussels, if using, and simmer gently until warmed through. Stir in the remaining 2 tablespoons of olive oil. Serve immediately or refrigerate to eat later, cold or reheated. Garnish with fresh cracked pepper just before serving.

LOBSTER BISQUE

SERVES 4 TO 6

A good bisque should taste deeply of shellfish and be silky smooth on the tongue. I like to sharpen these flavors by replacing the usual and sometimes plodding heavy cream with sour cream; the slight spike of acidity brings focus to this gregarious mélange. Bisque is a platform that accommodates any shellfish or fish. In place of lobster you might use shrimp, crayfish, steamed mussels, or blue crab with its roe.

2 quarts Shellfish Stock (page 96) or Basic Fish Stock (page 93)

10 allspice berries

4 whole cloves

1 bay leaf

2 (1¼-pound) lobsters, preferably new shell

8 tablespoons (1 stick) butter

4 carrots, chopped

2 stalks celery, chopped

2 onions, chopped

½ cup rice

2 tablespoons tomato paste

1 teaspoon ground mace

2 cups white wine

1 cup sour cream

2 tablespoons amontillado sherry or brandy

Combine the stock, allspice, cloves, and bay leaf, and bring to a boil. Add the lobsters, cover, and cook for 5 minutes. Remove from the heat.

Transfer the lobsters to a bowl to cool. Working over the bowl to catch all the juices, crack the shells to remove the meat; reserve. Return the shells and juices to the pot and simmer gently for 20 minutes. Remove from the heat and pour the fortified stock through a fine-mesh strainer; reserve.

Meanwhile, heat the butter in a separate large pot over medium-high heat. Add the carrots, celery, onion, and rice and cook, stirring occasionally, until the onion is soft, about 7 minutes. Stir in the tomato paste and mace, and cook until the tomato has darkened in color and its aroma has softened, 5 to 7 minutes.

Add the wine, bring to a boil, and boil for 4 minutes. Add the reserved stock, reduce the heat to low, and simmer gently until the rice is fully cooked, about 15 minutes.

Meanwhile, dice half of the reserved lobster meat and reserve for a garnish. Stir the remaining lobster meat into the stock and remove from the heat.

Transfer the soup to a blender, preferably a Vita-Prep. Working in batches, blend, gradually increasing the speed, until the mixture is very smooth and silky (always take care when blending hot liquids). Strain the soup though a fine-mesh strainer, pressing on the solids with the back of a ladle. Discard any solids that do not pass through.

Gently reheat the bisque if necessary. Just before serving, whisk in the sour cream and sherry. Divide the bisque among bowls and garnish with the reserved diced lobster meat. Serve immediately.

Sherry and Madeira

If your only knowledge of sherry is that old bottle of insipid cooking wine in your grandmother's cabinet, then you are truly missing out. Just as desserts are often finished with a dollop of whipped cream, or a great pasta is made perfect with a few shavings of Parmesan, sherry and Madeira wines can add just the right grace note to a dish, making it all come together. Both of these fortified wines, produced in many styles and levels of sweetness, add wonderful complexity to seafood soups and stews. Their nutty flavors lend depth while the slight sweetness and baked fruit aromas add an ethereal interest. The alcohol also provides an additional bite, which is especially deft at balancing rich bisques.

There is a long history in Southern cuisine using cream sherry to fortify soups such as she-crab, terrapin, or shrimp bisque, but I prefer more refined styles of sherry, such as amontillado and palo cortado. Madeira pairs particularly well with lightly spiced dishes such as Portuguese-Style Clam Chowder spiked with peppery linguiça sausage (page 108). I always have a bottle of both Rainwater and Verdelho styles of Madeira on hand in my kitchen, as much for sipping as for cooking. As good as these are when added to soups or stews, they are equally compelling sprinkled over fish fillets meant for the grill or the broiler. As the alcohol burns off, the fish is infused with the fruity perfume and acidity of the wine.

SPICED COCONUT BROTH WITH SHELLFISH

SERVES 4

This soup is incredibly versatile and able to adapt to almost any creative combination you dream up. Some of the coconut milk can be substituted with fish stock or wine for a more complex broth. Butternut squash adds an untraditional twist to this recipe; its earthy sweetness balances the citrusy broth.

24 littleneck clams or 2 pounds mussels, washed thoroughly (discard any open or damaged ones)

1 cup clam juice or white wine

2 (14-ounce) cans unsweetened coconut milk

1 cup water

1 stalk lemon grass, bruised with the flat end of a knife

2 strips lime or lemon zest

2 pods star anise

1 bay leaf

2 cups finely diced butternut squash (about 1 small squash)

2 plum tomatoes, cored and diced

¼ cup chopped cilantro

Pinch crushed red chile flakes

Salt

3 tablespoons almond or roasted peanut oil, optional

1 lime, cut in 4 wedges

Combine the clams and clam juice in a heavy pot, and heat over high heat. Cook, covered, until the clams open, 5 to 7 minutes. Remove from the heat and, working over the pot, pick out the clam meat and transfer to a bowl. Discard shells and any clams that haven't opened. Pour the cooking liquid through a fine mesh sieve into another pot, taking care to separate any grit left from the clams.

Add the coconut milk, water, lemon grass, lime zest, star anise, and bay leaf to the cooking liquid. Bring to a simmer over medium heat and cook for 20 minutes. Pluck out the lemon grass, lime zest, star anise, and bay leaf and discard.

Add the butternut squash and simmer until tender, 8 to 10 minutes. Add the tomatoes, cilantro, chile flakes, and the reserved clam meat and simmer gently until warmed through. Season with salt if needed. Divide the soup among four bowls, drizzle each with almond oil, if using, and serve with the lime wedges.

PORTUGUESE-STYLE CLAM CHOWDER

SERVES 4

Clam chowder can incite furious debate. Which is better—red or white? If the purpose of this argument isn't clear to you, you're not alone, because it really doesn't make any sense—they can both be delicious! This popular red chowder originated on the southern shores of Massachusetts, where a large Portuguese immigrant population built thriving fishing communities. Tomatoes, spicy linguiça sausage, a liberal seasoning of paprika, and the mandatory slug of nutty Madeira put this soup in a category all its own. If entertaining, make the broth ahead, then add the clams and finish just before serving.

5 tablespoons extra-virgin olive oil, divided use

2 tablespoons tomato paste

2 tablespoons smoked sweet paprika

2 sprigs fresh thyme

2 sprigs fresh oregano or marjoram, or 1½ teaspoons dried oregano

2 (14.5-ounce) cans fire-roasted tomatoes, plus 2 cans' worth of water

1 pound raw or cooked linguiça sausage, thinly sliced

1 bulb fennel, core removed and cut into ½-inch-thick dice

48 cockles or littleneck clams, scrubbed thoroughly to remove any grit

3 tablespoons Madeira, either Rainwater or Verdelho style

2 tablespoons red wine vinegar

Heat 3 tablespoons of the olive oil in a heavy pot over medium-high heat. Add the tomato paste and cook, stirring, for 5 minutes. Add the paprika, thyme, and oregano and cook until toasted and aromatic, about 1 minute. Add the canned tomatoes, water, sausage, and fennel. Bring to a simmer and cook until fennel is tender, about 15 minutes. (If making ahead of time, remove from the heat and refrigerate until ready to finish. Reheat gently before proceeding.)

Add the clams and increase the heat to high. Simmer vigorously until the clams open, 7 to 10 minutes. Discard any clams that don't open. Stir in the Madeira and vinegar. Divide among four bowls, drizzle with the remaining 2 tablespoons of olive oil, and serve.

FISH OR SHELLFISH PHO

SERVES 4

I take great liberties with this adaptation of the classic Vietnamese soup, but, in my defense, this version gets dinner on the table in minutes rather than hours and still delivers plenty of deep, exotic flavor. If you don't have homemade stock on hand, you can substitute store-bought vegetable stock.

8 cups Seagreen Stock (page 95), Basic Fish Stock (page 93), or Shellfish Stock (page 96)

2 (1-pound) lobsters

1 stalk celery, cut into 1-inch pieces

1-inch piece fresh ginger, peeled and sliced

1 tablespoon coriander seeds

10 allspice berries

8 whole cloves

4 bay leaves

Salt

8 ounces rice vermicelli

½ fresh hot chile pepper, such as serrano, jalapeño, or Fresno, cut into paper-thin rounds

4 sprigs basil, leaves gently torn

4 lime wedges

Heat the stock in a large pot. When it comes to a boil, add the lobsters, cover, and cook for 5 minutes. Transfer the lobsters to a bowl and set aside. Reduce the heat to a simmer. Add the celery, ginger, coriander, allspice, cloves, and bay leaves, and season with salt. Working over the bowl, remove the meat from the lobsters, reserving the shells and juice. Add the shells and juice back to the broth. Bring the broth to a simmer, then cover and turn off the heat. Let steep.

Meanwhile, slice the lobster into small bite-size pieces and set aside. Cook the noodles according to the package directions. Strain the broth and divide among four large bowls. Add the noodles to each bowl and top with the lobster pieces. Garnish with the sliced chile and basil, and serve with the lime wedges.

ZUPPA DI PESCE

SERVES 4 TO 6

The crown jewel of many a mom-and-pop Italian joint, a good *zuppa di pesce* should be made with crushed San Marzano tomatoes, lightly seasoned so as not to mask the freshness of the generous assortment of seafood called for. All you need to complete the meal is plenty of crusty bread—oh, and chilled light red wine!

½ cup olive oil

1 large fennel bulb, diced

3 cloves garlic, smashed

6 whole cloves

1 lemon, halved

3 strips orange zest

2 sprigs fresh thyme

1 spring fresh oregano, or 1 teaspoon dried oregano

1 (28-ounce) can crushed San Marzano tomatoes

Salt

4 cups Seagreen Stock (page 95), Shellfish Stock (page 96), or Basic Fish Stock (page 93)

1 pound mussels, well scrubbed

1 pound swordfish or other firm-fleshed fish such as dogfish or monkfish, cut into 2-inch pieces

1 pound mackerel fillets, cut into 2-inch pieces

1 pound Gulf shrimp, preferably head-on

Heat the olive oil in a large, wide pot over medium-high heat. Add the fennel and garlic and cook, stirring occasionally, until just wilted, 3 to 5 minutes. Poke the cloves into the skin of the lemon halves (3 cloves per lemon half). Add the clove-studded lemons to the pot, cut side down, along with the orange zest, thyme, and oregano. Cook until fragrant, about 3 minutes. Add the crushed tomatoes, season with salt, and bring to a boil. Add the stock and the mussels. Bring to an energetic simmer and cook until the mussels just begin to open. Nestle the swordfish and mackerel pieces into the liquid. Cover, reduce the heat to very low, and simmer for 10 minutes. Add the shrimp, cover, and cook for 5 minutes more. Remove from the heat and let sit, covered, for 20 minutes and up to an 1 hour, for the flavors to meld. Gently reheat and serve.

Stews

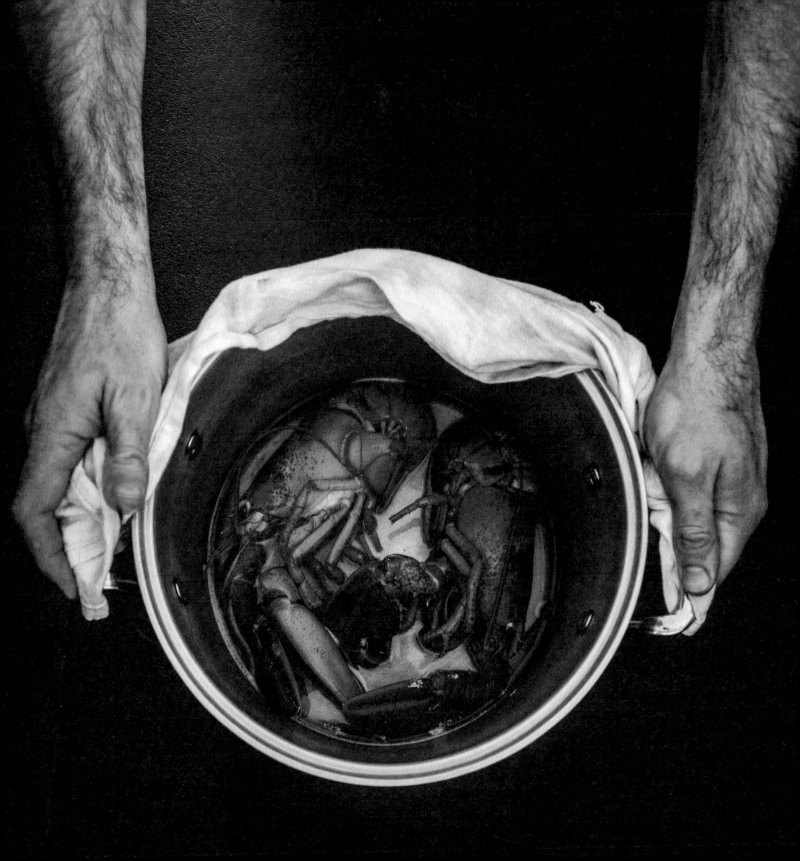

COTRIADE

SERVES 4 TO 6

This uniquely flavored stew, originating from the Bretagne region in northern France, has a fragrant earthy flair due to a mix of herbs including sage, a seasoning not often paired with seafood. As the combined flavors are somewhat autumnal, I like to include a few sweet and spicy root vegetables, which provide a handsome brace to the roux-thickened broth.

3 pounds mixed white-fleshed fish, such as monkfish, flounder, haddock, halibut, pollock, etc., cut into 1-inch cubes

Salt

1 pound mussels, well scrubbed, or shrimp, preferably head-on

6 cups Basic Fish Stock (page 93)

2 cups hard cider, preferably a drier style such as cidre de Normandie, or white wine

16 tablespoons (2 sticks) butter

2 sprigs fresh thyme

1 sprig fresh sage

2 strips lemon zest

10 saffron threads

1 cup flour

2 cups chopped butternut squash (1-inch cubes)

1 large celery root, peeled and cut into 1-inch cubes

1 fennel bulb, cut into thin wedges

10 to 15 radishes, scrubbed, halved if large

1 small leek, tough outer greens discarded, sliced into ½-inch rounds

3 shallots, cut into 8 wedges each

¼ cup chopped fresh tarragon leaves

½ bunch flat-leaf parsley, leaves only, chopped

Season the fish with salt and let sit for 10 minutes to help firm up the flesh. Combine the fish, mussels, stock, and cider in a large pot over medium heat. Gradually bring to a simmer, then cook until the mussels open, 3 to 5 minutes. Gently remove the seafood and set aside. Strain the stock into a bowl and reserve.

Heat the butter in the cleaned pot over medium heat. Add the thyme, sage, and lemon zest, and cook until aromatic, about 5 minutes. Add the saffron. Sift the flour into the pot, whisking to ensure no clumps form. Cook the roux, stirring frequently, until it is light brown, about 10 minutes. Add the reserved stock and whisk to combine. Add the squash, celery root, fennel, radishes, leek, and shallots and cook until the squash is tender and the broth is lightly thickened, about 30 minutes.

Discard the thyme and sage sprigs. Return the fish and mussels to the broth and simmer gently until heated through. Taste for seasoning and adjust with salt if needed. Add the tarragon and parsley and serve immediately.

BOUILLABAISSE

SERVES 6 TO 8

The term *bouillabaisse* is derived from the regional French Occitan dialect and translates roughly to "layer and boil." The hallmark of the dish is the inclusion of a huge variety (some swear it must be 12 kinds) of different seafood, all poached in turn in a stock. With each variety the stock becomes ever more flavorful and complex. Not surprisingly, there are almost as many interpretations of this dish as there are fish in the pot. Some cooks like to serve the seafood presented on a platter and the cooking broth in a tureen to be ladled separately. My bouillabaisse includes lots of vegetables and spices, the result being more of a chunky stew than a soupy broth and is best served altogether in the same bowl. I also take up the tradition of adding the romantic scent of herbes de Provence and finishing the soup with a slug of Pernod.

Bouillabaisse is usually served with a dab of rouille (page 262), an emulsified and spiced paste of bread and garlic, but I prefer the simplicity of aioli. If you want to mimic the flavors of rouille, simply add a pinch of cayenne and a few strands of saffron to the aioli.

6 tablespoons olive oil

3 tablespoons butter

4 stalks celery, cut into ½-inch pieces

4 large shallots, sliced into ¼-inch-thick rings

1 large fennel bulb, finely diced

2 cloves garlic, smashed

1 bay leaf

4 tablespoons tomato paste

1 tablespoon herbes de Provence

1 tablespoon smoked sweet paprika

2 teaspoons crushed red chile flakes

2 cups white wine

2½ quarts Basic Fish Stock (page 93) or Shellfish Stock (page 96)

1 pound small red potatoes, cut into bite-size pieces

Salt

1 lemon, halved

24 cockles or littleneck clams, scrubbed

1 pound mussels, scrubbed

2 pounds mixed fresh fish, such as halibut, red snapper, black sea bass, and monkfish, preferably on the bone

8 ounces Gulf shrimp, preferably head-on, shells removed

8 ounces medium scallops, untreated or dry pack

4 capfuls Pernod

1 baguette, sliced

Garlic for perfuming the toast (page 119)

Classic Aioli, for serving (page 257)

Combine the olive oil and butter in a large stew pot over medium heat. Add the celery, shallots, fennel, smashed garlic, and bay leaf, and cook for 10 minutes.

Stir in the tomato paste, herbes de Provence, paprika, and chile flakes and cook until the tomato paste is a shade darker, 3 to 5 minutes. Add the wine and cook until the alcohol has dissipated, about 3 minutes. Add the fish stock and potatoes and season with salt. Bring to a boil, then add the lemon halves and the clams, cover the pot, and cook until the clams have opened, 5 to 7 minutes. Discard any shells that haven't opened.

Add the mussels, cover, and cook until the mussels have opened, 3 to 5 minutes. Discard any shells that haven't opened. Reduce the heat to low, and add the fish, shrimp, and scallops. Cover the pot and simmer gently until the shrimp are fully cooked and the seafood begins to flake apart, 7 to 10 minutes. Gently stir in the Pernod and remove from the heat. Cover and let rest for 10 to 15 minutes.

Meanwhile, toast the baguette slices and rub each piece with the garlic halves. Serve the bouillabaisse in large bowls with the garlic toast and aioli on the side.

Herbes de Provence

Herbes de Provence is a potent spice blend with a rugged, wild personality. It typically includes dried oregano, rosemary, thyme, savory, and, in many cases, a small amount of lavender, and it is very evocative of the landscape for which it is named. Its character can easily overwhelm a dish, so exercise caution—a little goes a long way. Blend a pinch of herbes de Provence with olive oil and balsamic vinegar as a dip for bread or rub onto steaks and pork before grilling. When paired with seafood, it is best to tame its vigor by infusing it into an oil (page 228) to be used as an aromatic finishing drizzle. This is especially good on salmon and grilled fish.

Rubbing Toast with Garlic

It's not hard to make toast—hey, you've been making it your whole life, right?—but it's incredibly simple to make it unforgettable. As soon as the bread is toasted to your preferred degree of crispness, take halved garlic cloves and rub each slice of toast with the cut side of the garlic. Just a few passes over the craggy surface of the warm bread will draw out and soften the aromatic oils of the garlic. The result is a whiff of spicy garlic essence. This dramatic and simple improvement takes but a few seconds, and this fragrant toast makes a terrific accompaniment to soups, stews, and salads. (I do not recommend this technique for breakfast toast!)

Boiling Garlic

Garlic can really make or break a dish. I find that boiling garlic cloves before using them helps their flavor to shine while tempering their potentially ill effects. The process is very simple: Place the needed number of cloves in a small pot and cover with cold water. Bring to a boil and then drain. Repeat this process two more times and you're all set. At this point, the boiled cloves have all of the nutty aroma, hint of spice, and charming sweetness that you want from raw garlic and can be used the same way. The boiled cloves are an especially good addition to pestos in which the flavor of garlic can become overwhelming after just a few hours.

CIOPPINO

SERVES 4 TO 6

This American fish stew, which originated in San Francisco, usually includes Dungeness crabs, clams, and sand dabs, a small flatfish similar to flounder. I have eaten countless versions of this dish in countless restaurants in the Bay Area, and I still get giddy when I see a big steaming bowl heading my way with giant Dungeness crab halves poking out from the broth. The whole thing can get a little messy, so come prepared with extra napkins and a bowl for the shells.

¼ cup extra-virgin olive oil

4 slices thick-cut bacon

2 small onions, cut into wedges
(leave root intact)

2 small bulbs fennel, cut into
wedges

4 garlic cloves, minced

4 sprigs fresh thyme

2 sprigs fresh oregano or
1 teaspoon dried oregano

1 teaspoon crushed
red chile flakes

2 tablespoons tomato paste

1 (28-ounce) can crushed
tomatoes

1 cup white wine

2 cups bottled clam juice or
Basic Fish Stock (page 93)

1 bay leaf

2 Dungeness crabs, cooked and
split in half

Salt

1 pound whitefish, such as
haddock, Pollock, or cod,
cut into bite-size pieces

24 littleneck clams, scrubbed

1 pound mussels, scrubbed

1¼ pounds shrimp, shell-on

1 bunch flat-leaf parsley,
leaves chopped

3 sprigs basil, leaves torn

Toasted sourdough bread,
for serving

Garlic for perfuming the
toast (page 119)

Heat the oil with the bacon in a very large pot over medium heat. Cook the bacon until rendered and crisp. Transfer the bacon to a paper towel–lined plate to drain. When it is cool, finely chop the bacon and reserve.

Add the onions and fennel to the pot and cook until the onion is translucent, about 10 minutes. Add the minced garlic, thyme, oregano and chile flakes, and cook for 2 minutes. Stir in the tomato paste and cook 3 to 5 minutes. Add the tomatoes with their juices, wine, clam juice, and bay leaf. Add the crabs and season with salt. Reduce the heat to medium-low, cover, and simmer until the flavors blend and the crabs heat through, about 30 minutes. Remove from the heat and let sit for a few hours for flavors to meld (or refrigerate overnight).

Return the pot to a simmer. Lightly season the whitefish with salt and set aside. Add the clams and mussels to the cooking liquid, cover, and cook until the clams and mussels begin to open, 5 to 7 minutes. Add the shrimp and fish. Simmer gently until the fish and shrimp are just cooked through, gently stirring from time to time, about 5 minutes longer (discard any clams and mussels that do not open).

Stir in the parsley, basil, and reserved bacon. Remove from the heat and let sit, covered, for 10 to 20 minutes. Divide among bowls and serve with the toasted sourdough bread rubbed with garlic.

BURRIDA

SERVES 4 TO 6

I first came across this dish on a cool autumn afternoon while traveling in Italy. I was taking a late lunch at a café in a coastal village while a salty fog stumbled over itself on its march toward the shore. The white broth, punctuated with meaty chunks of white fish and shrimp, had been thickened with a purée of toasted almonds and butter. I loved this rich finishing touch; it was new to me and somehow fit the leisurely afternoon's mood so perfectly.

1 cup slivered blanched almonds

8 tablespoons (1 stick) butter

Finely grated zest of 1 lemon

1 teaspoon ground mace

Salt

6 tablespoons extra-virgin olive oil

4 stalks celery, chopped into ½-inch pieces

2 carrots, chopped into ½-inch pieces

1 fennel bulb, chopped into ½-inch pieces

1 leek, chopped

3 cloves garlic, chopped

1 (2-ounce) can oil-packed anchovies

6 cups Basic Fish Stock (page 93)

2 pounds white fish, such as haddock, Pollock, halibut, sablefish, or cod, cut into 1-inch pieces

1 pound Gulf shrimp, preferably head-on, shelled

2 tablespoons sherry

Baguette, for serving

Preheat the oven to 325°F.

Arrange the almonds on a small baking sheet and toast in the oven, stirring occasionally, until they just begin to brown, about 10 minutes. Cool completely.

Using a food processor or mortar and pestle, grind the almonds to a paste. Add the butter, lemon zest, and mace, and season with salt. Grind until the mixture is a fine purée, about 1 minute. Reserve.

Heat the olive oil in a large, heavy stew pot over high heat. Add the celery, carrot, fennel, leek, and garlic, and cook, undisturbed, for about 5 minutes. Give the vegetables a stir and continue to cook until lightly browned and beginning to crisp, about 5 minutes more. Add the anchovies with their oil and cook until the anchovies disintegrate into the vegetables, about 2 minutes. Add the stock and bring to a simmer.

Season the fish with salt. Add the fish and shrimp, reduce the heat to low, and simmer until just cooked through 8 to 10 minutes. Taste for seasoning and adjust as needed. Using a slotted spoon, transfer the fish and vegetables to large bowls. Bring the broth to a full boil, then add the reserved almond butter and whisk vigorously to combine. Boil until the broth is slightly thickened, 3 to 5 minutes. Stir in the sherry. Ladle the broth over the seafood and vegetables and serve with slices of baguette.

BOURRIDE

SERVES 4 TO 6

Bourride distinguishes itself with its gutsy flavorings—a combination of flowery fennel, snarling ginger, smoky paprika, and the delicate perfume of saffron, which tints the broth a rusty, sunset orange. The stew's real kicker is the aioli that is whisked in just before serving. The resulting broth is rich and velvety and lends the wealth of fish and vegetables a delicious sheen.

½ cup olive oil

3 small fennel bulbs, cut into wedges

1 large onion, finely chopped

3 (¼-inch-thick) slices fresh ginger

4 tablespoons butter

1 tablespoon smoked sweet paprika

Pinch saffron threads (about 10)

2 cups white wine

2 pounds mixed white fish, such as snapper, flounder, haddock, or rockfish, cut into 1-inch pieces

Salt

2½ quarts Basic Fish Stock (page 93)

¼ cup red wine vinegar

1 fresh chile pepper, such as Fresno or jalapeño, halved (optional)

1 pound mussels, scrubbed, any broken or open shells discarded

½ pound bay or other small scallops, dry packed or untreated

½ pound Gulf shrimp, preferably head-on, shelled

2 cups Classic Aioli (page 257)

2 tablespoons amontillado sherry

2 tablespoons chopped chives

Toasted baguette slices, for serving

Heat the olive oil in a large, heavy stew pot over high heat. Add the fennel, onion, and ginger, and cook for 5 minutes. Add the butter, paprika, and saffron, and cook until the butter is melted and the spices are toasted, about 3 minutes. Add the wine and bring to a boil.

Season the fish with salt. Add the fish stock, vinegar, and chile pepper, if using, and season with salt. Add the mussels and boil until they open, 3 to 5 minutes. Reduce the heat to low and add the fish, scallops, and shrimp, and simmer until just cooked through, 10 to 15 minutes. Remove from the heat.

Gently ladle most of the broth out into a separate pan, keeping the fish covered in the original pan. Heat the broth to a simmer and add the aioli, whisking quickly to combine. Reduce the heat to low and cook until the broth begins to thicken, 3 to 5 minutes. Stir in the sherry and chopped chives. Divide the seafood and vegetables among four bowls. Ladle the aioli-thickened broth over the seafood and vegetables. Serve with toasted baguette slices.

RAITO

SERVES 4 TO 6

Traditionally served on Christmas Eve in parts of Italy, this seafood stew is defined by its thickener of pounded walnuts and butter, flavored with rosemary. This assertive herb is not often paired with seafood, but here a healthy dose of red wine tempers its woodsy scent. This unique dish is just the thing for a cold winter's night.

2 pounds white fish, such as bass, haddock, halibut, or sablefish, cut into 1-inch pieces

1 pound squid, cut into small rings

Salt

6 cups Basic Fish Stock (page 93)

12 tablespoons butter, divided use

2 onions, each cut into eight wedges (leave the root intact so they hold together)

2 fennel bulbs, cut into wedges

1 sprig fresh rosemary

2 tablespoons capers, rinsed and drained

2 dried chile peppers or 1 tablespoon crushed red chile flakes

1 bay leaf

2 cups red wine

1 cup walnut pieces

1 clove garlic, grated on a Microplane grater

Finely grated zest of 1 lemon

1 teaspoon ground mace

1 pound mussels or 12 clams, scrubbed

3 plum tomatoes, cored and small diced

Season the fish and squid with salt. Heat the stock in a large pan over medium heat until steaming. Add the fish and squid pieces, cover, and gently poach until they are cooked through, 7 to 10 minutes. Remove from the heat. Gently transfer the seafood to a tray. Reserve the seafood and broth separately.

Melt 6 tablespoons of the butter in a large pot over medium-high heat. Add the onions, fennel, rosemary, capers, chiles, and bay leaf. Cook, stirring occasionally, until the vegetables begin to soften, 5 to 7 minutes.

Add the wine and bring to a boil. Add the reserved stock, reduce the heat to low, and simmer for 10 minutes.

While the soup cooks, grind the walnuts to a paste using a food processor or mortar and pestle. Add the remaining 6 tablespoons of butter, garlic, lemon zest, and mace, and season with salt. Grind until the mixture is a fine purée, about 1 minute.

Add the walnut butter to the pot, stirring gently to incorporate. Add the mussels and bring to a boil. Cook until the mussels begin to open and the broth is slightly thickened, about 5 minutes. Add the tomato and the reserved fish and squid and cover the pot. Remove from the heat and allow the stew to rest, covered, for 10 to 15 minutes. Divide the fish among warmed bowls. Pour the broth and vegetables over the top and serve with crusty bread.

GUMBO

SERVES 4 TO 6

There are more gumbos than there are cooks in the South, and each and every one is authentic in its own way. The nature of this dish is complex and curious, its flavors and textures as vivid as the wild characters that stand over those pots stirring it up and telling tales. I love this particular mixture of meaty chicken thighs, andouille sausage, and shrimp swimming in a well-spiced sauce. Its flavors become even more interesting if made ahead and allowed to sit overnight.

2 pounds bone-in, skin-on chicken thighs

Salt

8 tablespoons (1 stick) butter, divided use

1 pound andouille sausage, cut into 1-inch pieces

3 stalks celery, finely diced

1 large onion, finely diced

1 green bell pepper, finely diced

1 fennel bulb, cut into eight wedges

3 cloves garlic, smashed

1 tablespoon crushed red chile flakes

1 bay leaf

½ cup flour

1 bottle dark beer

3 tablespoons Worcestershire sauce

6 cups Basic Fish Stock (page 93), Shellfish Stock (page 96), or chicken stock

1 pound okra, cut in thirds on a bias

1 (28-ounce) can diced fire-roasted tomatoes

1 lemon, halved

1 pound Gulf shrimp

Steamed white rice, for serving

Season the chicken thighs with salt. Melt 3 tablespoons of the butter in a heavy-bottomed stew pot over high heat. Add the chicken and sear, skin side down, until well browned, about 5 minutes. Add the sausage and cook until it begins to color, about 5 minutes. Transfer the meats to a bowl and reserve.

Reduce the heat to medium and add 1 tablespoon of the remaining butter to the pan. Add the celery, onion, bell pepper, fennel, garlic, chile flakes, and bay leaf, and season with salt. Cook, stirring occasionally, until the vegetables are aromatic and softened, about 8 minutes.

Using a slotted spoon, transfer the vegetables to a bowl, leaving any butter and sausage oil in the pan. Melt the remaining 4 tablespoons of butter in the pan, then add the flour and stir to combine. Cook the roux over medium heat, stirring constantly with a wooden spoon, until golden brown, about 8 minutes.

Add the beer and Worcestershire sauce to the roux, stirring until smooth and combined. Stir in the stock. Add the okra, tomatoes, lemon halves, and the reserved vegetables. Return the chicken and sausage to the pan, then add the shrimp. Bring the mixture to a boil, then reduce the heat to low, cover, and simmer until thickened, about 1 hour. Check seasoning and adjust if needed.

Serve over steamed rice.

PACIFIC STEW

SERVES 4 TO 6

The rich broth and warm flavors of this stew are the perfect match for salmon. The roasted garlic and rosemary are what really set this dish apart, but feel free to change up the seasonality of this stew: substitute butternut squash for the zucchini, throw in some roasted onions, and use hardier herbs, such as thyme. Like so many stews, this one tastes even better the next day.

6 tablespoons butter, divided use

6 to 8 cloves roasted garlic

2 small onions, cut into wedges

1 fresh chile pepper, such as Fresno, sliced

1 sprig fresh rosemary

1 pound red potatoes, cut into 1-inch pieces

2 roasted red peppers, cut into 1-inch strips

1 cup red wine

2 (14-ounce) cans diced, peeled tomatoes

2 zucchini, cut into ½-inch pieces

18 clams, scrubbed

6 cups Basic Fish Stock (page 93)

Salt

1½ pounds salmon, cut into 2-inch pieces

1 pound white fish, such as Pollock, Pacific rockfish, halibut, or sablefish, cut into 1-inch pieces

4 tablespoons chopped fresh herbs, such as tarragon, parsley, or chives

2 tablespoons Madeira

Baguette, for serving

Heat 2 tablespoons of the butter in a large stew pot over medium heat. Add the roasted garlic, onion, chile, and rosemary. Toss to coat, and cook 5 minutes. Add the potatoes, roasted peppers, and red wine. Bring to a boil and cook until most of the wine has evaporated. Add the tomatoes, zucchini, clams, and stock. Season with salt. Bring to a boil and cook until the potatoes are just tender and the clams have opened, about 10 minutes. Discard any clams that haven't opened.

Season the salmon and white fish with salt. Add the fish to the stew and return to a simmer. Immediately cover and remove from the heat. Let sit, covered, for at least 10 to 15 minutes. Just before serving, gently stir in the herbs, Madeira, and remaining 4 tablespoons of butter. Serve with slices of baguette.

VIRGINIA STEW

SERVES 4 TO 6

Although there are many chowders and stews similar to this one, I call it a Virginia stew because it is chock-full of ingredients familiar from my childhood near the Old Dominion. Like most stews, this one benefits from being made ahead. If using true country ham, make sure to boil it first to rehydrate it.

8 tablespoons (1 stick) butter

8 ounces country ham (preferably 2 thick slices), diced

3 stalks celery, diced

1 onion, diced

1 red bell pepper, diced

6 cups Basic Fish Stock (page 93), Shellfish Stock (page 96), or chicken stock

1 cup clam juice

6 ripe plum tomatoes (about 1 pound), cored and each cut into 8 wedges

2 ears corn, cut into 1-inch rounds

1 fennel bulb, diced

4 sprigs fresh thyme

2 bay leaves

Salt

1 pound flounder fillets, boneless and skinless

2 dozen small clams, scrubbed

1 pound lump blue crabmeat, picked

2 tablespoons amontillado sherry

Cornbread or biscuits, for serving

Heat the butter in a large, heavy stew pot over high heat. Add the ham, celery, onion, and bell pepper and cook, stirring occasionally, until the ham begins to brown and the vegetables wilt, 8 to 10 minutes. Add the stock, clam juice, tomatoes, corn, fennel, thyme, and bay leaves, and season with salt. Reduce the heat to low, cover, and simmer for 20 minutes.

Meanwhile, season the flounder with salt and let sit for 10 minutes.

Increase the heat to high. Add the clams and cook, covered, until they open, 7 to 10 minutes. Reduce the heat to low and nestle the flounder into the cooking liquid until submerged, then add the crabmeat. Cover the pot, remove from the heat, and let sit for at least 20 minutes before serving. Stir in the sherry. Serve with cornbread or biscuits.

GREEN CURRY FISH STEW

SERVES 4 TO 6

Fresh and bright, this green curry stew gets its creaminess from cashews. Serving it with lime and yogurt not only cools some of the heat but also heightens the flavors through a burst of acidity.

3 cups Basic Fish Stock (page 93), or a mixture of clam juice and water

10 small red potatoes, halved

1 cup raw cashews

1 stalk lemon grass, bruised with the heel of a knife

1 bay leaf

1 pod star anise

Salt

1 bunch cilantro, leaves only

1 bunch flat-leaf parsley, leaves only

1 fresh chile pepper, thinly sliced

Juice of 1 lime

4 tablespoons butter

1 tablespoon ground cumin

1 tablespoon ground coriander

1 onion, grated

1 fennel bulb, grated

2 garlic cloves, grated

A ½-inch piece of ginger, grated

1½ pounds white fish fillets, such as haddock, pollock, hake, rockfish, halibut, or catfish, cut into 1-inch pieces

1 lime, cut into wedges, for serving

Yogurt, to garnish (optional)

Combine the fish stock, potatoes, cashews, lemon grass, bay leaf, and star anise in a pot. Season with salt and bring to a simmer over medium heat. Simmer until the potatoes are just tender, 12 to 15 minutes. Remove from the heat. Using a slotted spoon, transfer the potatoes to a bowl and reserve. Pluck out and discard the lemon grass, bay leaf, and star anise. Transfer the broth and cashews to a blender. Add the cilantro, parsley, and chile, and purée until very smooth (use caution when blending hot liquids). Add the lime juice and some additional fish stock, if needed, to thin the mixture to a smooth purée. Set aside.

Heat the butter in the same pot over medium heat. Add the cumin and coriander and cook, stirring, until toasted and fragrant, about 1 minute. Add the grated onion, fennel, garlic, and ginger, and cook 5 to 6 minutes. Stir in the reserved cashew sauce.

Season the fish with salt and let sit for 5 minutes. Nestle the potatoes into the sauce to create "beds," then place the fish on the beds. Reduce the heat to low and simmer until fish is cooked through, about 5 minutes. Serve the stew with the lime wedges and a dollop of yogurt, if desired.

SEAGREENS

Many of us are familiar with seaweeds as part of a meal out at a sushi joint—the nori in our California rolls, neon-green seaweed salad, steaming bowls of miso soup flavored with dashi and wakame—but there is an immense array of other seaweeds out there. In fact, seaweeds are a giant global industry, topping $7 billion per year, with the vast majority produced in Asia. Seaweeds offer an incredible culinary opportunity and are well worth exploring. Happily, there is an emerging industry for this environmentally restorative and delicious superfood here in North America.

Seaweeds, also known as seagreens or sea vegetables, are algae, a very large and diverse group of organisms that are distantly related to plants. The number of species in this group is estimated to be in the billions. There are two groups of algae: micro (the film that grows on ponds) and macro (large varieties we know from the coasts). And while algae grow in both freshwater and saltwater, for culinary purposes, I will only explore a few of the saltwater varieties of macro-algae that are currently being produced for our tables. Let's call them seagreens from this point on.

Seagreens are pretty wacky in how they grow. They do not need to grow roots because their cells absorb nutrients directly from to the surrounding water (as opposed to plants, that absorb nutrients from the soil through their roots) Like plants, algae are photosynthetic and require sunlight in order to live; thus their range is typically found near the shore, where light penetrates the water. In many cases, when the tides roll out, seagreens may gain direct exposure to life-sustaining light.

There is a enduring and storied history of seagreens used in shore-side cooking. The great New England clam and lobster bakes, for instance, rely on seagreens to help provide that unique coastal flavor. While each bake master practices his or her own unique method, the basic idea is to steam a generous collection of shellfish—clams, lobsters, and mussels, for example—over a slow, soulful fire. The first step is to gather up driftwood and build up a fire in a deep pit in the sand. Once the fire has burned down to smoldering embers, seagreens are laid over the top. Then, a bounty of seafoods and vegetables, including lobsters, clams, mussels, potatoes, corn, and sausage, is nestled into the now steamy fire pit. Another layer of seagreens is laid over the top, capturing the food in a smoky sea sauna. The principal seagreen used for this tradition is rockweed, prized for its sea-brine tang and the rich flavor it imparts to foods.

Here is a list of seagreens products currently and commonly available in both traditional and specialty stores. In addition, almost any seagreen can easily be ordered online.

Umami

Around 1910, Japanese scientist Kikunae Ikeda identified a "fifth taste," a naturally occurring flavor found in many foods that was distinct from the already familiar sweet, sour, bitter, and salty flavors. He referred to his discovery as umami, which translates roughly to "delicious taste" or "pleasant savory taste." Umami is present in many common foods, such as mushrooms, soy sauce, and Parmesan cheese. It is especially prevalent in seagreens.

The Kelps, aka Kombu

Kelps make up the majority of brown algae species.

WINGED KELP, *Alaria esculenta*

This beautiful, thick-ribbed seagreen is found in the intertidal and near-shore areas. With a palm frond–like shape, winged kelp is mostly sold in dried form and is best used to add a subtle and nuanced flavor to dashi broth or other broths or stews. Though commonly known as kombu, it is also called alaria and Atlantic wakame, but my favorite alias is lady kelp. Winged kelp is high in umami content, and it coaxes a boldness from all other ingredients with which it is paired. When the dried product is rehydrated, it becomes a lovely addition to salads—its snappy texture provides contrast to softer greens. When adding winged kelp to salads, I like to rehydrate it with vinegar, as the acidity integrates seamlessly into the sea-brine tang of the greens. The dried product is also good simply crumbled over dishes such as roasted vegetables or autumn soups.

WAKAME, *Undaria pinnatifida*

Wakame makes up the bulk of the familiar bright green seaweed salad we know from sushi restaurants. Its glowing color is achieved by lightly salting the blanched blades of the seaweed (beware of food coloring used as a shortcut). Like many seagreens, wakame shows an affinity for the flavors of Asian cuisine, specifically ginger, garlic, and sesame. As a departure from the ubiquitous salad preparation, I like to crumble toasted wakame strands over salads or dishes like roasted broccoli.

SUGAR KELP, *Saccharina latissima*

Sugar kelp is the most commonly available seagreen and is, in my opinion, the easiest to introduce into our culinary repertoire, being both very easy to use and so mildly flavored. Its high natural sugars give this seagreen an herbal and fruity hint. Sugar kelp is both harvested wild and farmed in North America, and is available fresh, frozen, or dried. This seagreen is likely to emerge as the leading product as our domestic industry matures.

Sugar kelp also goes by the name kombu and is the principal variety I use for broths such as dashi. After rehydrating, the leaves can be finely chopped to use as a garnish for the finished soup. Sugar kelp fronds can grow to be very thick, and when dried and rehydrated they regain a pleasant texture and crunch, similar to a green bean. They make a wonderful addition to salads. Sugar kelp pairs particularly well with the spicy kick of raw onions, which flatters the mellow flavor of this seagreen and brings its sea charisma into focus.

ROCKWEED, *Fucus vesiculosus*

Rockweed, a member of the brown algae family (but not a kelp), is likely the most recognizable seagreen. Also known as bladderwrack, it is very common around beaches—you'll know it by its frilly, flowerlike fronds punctuated by small air bubbles that keep it afloat. Rockweed is harvested from the wild and is best known for its role in clambakes and lobster boils. The fronds release a heavy perfume that graces the seafood with a jolt of umami and salt. Boiling sausages, potatoes, and corn with this seagreen elevates their personalities and brings summer into full flavor. I also use dried rockweed for smoking meats and seafoods. Its briny driftwood smoke and cherry-mahogany color imparts a unique beachy flavor to meats and seafoods. Rockweed is not often used for direct consumption. Only its very tender tips have culinary merit—sautéed in a little bit of butter, for example, or fried in light cornmeal or a tempura batter. Rockweed often accompanies live lobsters when they are shipped beyond the coast, so it is worth asking your fishmonger if he can get some for you.

DULSE, *Palmaria palmata*

With its lovely violet-hued sheen; dense, leathery texture; and deep, rustic savor, dulse is one of the most versatile of all the seagreens. Dried, it displays a dark and brooding flavor (think dark chocolate); it definitely needs some partner ingredients to help balance it. A sprinkle of dulse flakes does wonders for dishes such as minestrone, bringing a mélange of ingredients into clear focus. Dulse sheets crisp nicely into chips and make a great snack—either dry roast the sheets or toast in a sauté pan with a touch of butter. Dulse is widely available from the Maine Coast Sea Vegetables company in multiple forms: as flakes, dried leaves, and leaves dried over a smoldering applewood fire (my favorite). Dulse is also a good source of protein, enabling it to substitute for meat. Dulse broths are well flavored and best used in such hearty dishes as beef stew or lentil soup. If you were to braise shortribs, for example, I think you'd be better off using a dulse broth than any other kind of stock.

LAVER, *Porphyra umbilicalis*

This intertidal seagreen is best known as nori, used as the wrappers for maki sushi. The variety grown in North America is called Atlantic nori, which is a different species than Japanese nori. The two can be used interchangeably. Laver is the among the most nutritious of the seagreens, containing vitamins B_1, B_6, B_{12}, C, and E, as well as protein, fiber, iron, and other minerals and trace elements.

In addition to making sushi, I crumble dried nori over and into salads, especially fruit salads. Try it with watermelon—nori's briny umami tang makes an explosive counterpoint to the sweet, juicy melon. Because this dried seagreen softens rapidly, it is best to add it at the last minute. Nori has recently become very popular as a snack item sold in thin strips flavored with a host of seasonings. Many people think of nori as a "gateway" seagreen because its flavors and textures are so accessible. Nori sheets are pleasantly elastic in bite, although after the initial snap, it has a wonderfully chewy texture, not unlike that of a fruit leather. Nori is mild and nutty in flavor, a quality enhanced by dry toasting the sheets in a sauté pan.

SEA LETTUCE, *Ulva lactuca*

This pastel green, delicately textured seagreen has a deep, rich flavor with a briny kick. When toasted in an low oven or sautéed in butter or (even better) bacon fat, the flavor softens and becomes a delightfully chewy snack or garnish for a main dish. Sea lettuce flakes easily pass for dried oregano, and, as a rule of thumb, any recipe that calls for dried oregano is made extremely interesting when sea lettuce flakes replace half the quantity of the brash herb. Sea lettuce is a very nice touch when a small amount is added to a classic Creole seasoning. Blasphemy, I know, but damn good nonetheless.

Seagreen Buying Guide

DRIED SEAGREENS

Dried seagreens are readily available. Once you start looking for them, you'll find them everywhere, from your local health food store to big box grocery stores! If you can't find the one you're looking for, ask your local store to stock it or order it online.

It is important to reinvigorate the character, texture, and flavor of dried seagreens by rehydrating them. This is essential if using seagreens as part of a raw preparation, such as a salad or marinated dish. Almost any liquid, such as vinegar, citrus, or wine, can be used to refresh the seagreens and introduce desired flavors. To rehydrate, simmer enough water to cover the seagreens. Add any flavorings you care to employ, such as star anise, white wine, and so on. Pour the liquid over the seagreens and ensure that they are fully submerged in the liquid. You may need to weigh them down with a plate. Check the seagreens after 15 minutes to see if they are plump all the way through. If they need more time, resubmerge them and check again every 5 minutes or so until done. When they are ready, drain the liquid and reserve it for another use if desired.

FRESH/FROZEN

Fresh and frozen seagreens are, for all culinary purposes, equal. This product form is just beginning to gain a foothold in the marketplace. It is not as versatile as the dried product in that it does not make great broths, but its fresh character and volume make it a great addition to traditional leafy green salads.

SUBSTITUTING DRIED SEAGREENS FOR FRESH (AND VICE VERSA)

As many recipes including seagreens can use either fresh or dried and rehydrated product, the simple calculation is that 2 ounces of dried seagreens will equal about 1 pound of fresh or frozen product.

USES AND PREPARATIONS

Think of seagreens this way: Kelp is the new kale! Given our familiarity with the generic idea of "a broad leafy vegetable," it is easy to imagine hundreds of ways to integrate these delicious and healthy ingredients into our culinary landscape. For instance, just imagine a rich lasagna layered with silken ricotta and briny sugar kelp, or a sauté of seagreens with smoky bacon, onions, and apples splashed with vinegar to bring it all together. Start by substituting seagreens for kale, collards, spinach, or chard in recipes you already know and love. You'll soon be branching out and getting more creative. There is no punishment involved with seagreens, only discovery.

FARMING AND HARVESTING SEAGREENS

Seagreen farming requires zero input. Fertilizers are unnecessary because seagreens take nutrients directly from the water in which they grow. This has the added benefits of maintaining the balance and resilience of coastal waterways and allowing high yields, all while keeping infrastructure and production costs low. Growth rates of seagreens can also be much greater than their landlocked counterparts, as the entirety of their energy is spent in growing, rather than in competing against natural forces, such as gravity.

Seagreens are an essential player in Earth's ecosystem. We often think of seagreens as solely a product of the shoreline, clinging to rocks as the tide

wild harvest of these seagreens, sometimes practiced sustainably and sometimes not, these algae grow very rapidly, making them ideal products to be farmed. In the United States, the farmed seaweed industry is just getting under way, and there are some wonderful products coming to a market near you.

Sugar kelp, a fast-maturing species that is not only sustainable but also restorative to the environments in which it is grown, is one of the major products now harvested. Sugar kelp absorbs excess carbon dioxide from the atmosphere and also gobbles up excess nitrogen in the water that spills into our waterways from our seaside communities. Nitrogen is a natural occurrence and its presence is essential, but when a coastline is paved over or stream banks eroded it is not able to be absorbed by the land and thus flushes into the sea. If unchecked, these marine ecosystems can become overnutrified. An excess of natural nutrients is not the same thing as dangerous pollution. Too much of any nutrient load in the water creates imbalances in the system. Farming seagreens brings these systems back into balance as they thrive with the ready availability of the nutrients vital for their growth.

The farming of seagreens also provides a bit of hope for fishing communities that have been in decline for many decades. This emerging economy offers an opportunity for fishermen to diversify their business and to use their knowledge, boats, and infrastructure to help sustain the fishing communities that have for so long put food on our tables. Efforts to increase production are centered in the Gulf of Maine, and this expanding industry, led by Maine Sea Grant and spearheaded by a brilliant young scientist, Sarah Redmond, has made converts out of oyster farmers, lobstermen, and fishermen alike.

shifts. But seagreens also grow in immense forests in water hundreds of feet deep. Growing dozens, if not hundreds of feet long, the fronds sway gently in the currents and provide an essential habitat for countless sea creatures. In it, juvenile fish find a safe place to hide from predators as they grow, while countless shellfish and other creatures find permanent homes.

There is great, and warranted, concern about the sustainability of the foods we take from the oceans. While many stories we hear tell of our depleted ecosystems and the greatly reduced number of fish in the seas, the story of seagreens is one worth celebrating. Seagreens exist naturally in the oceans, provide habitat for small and large marine creatures, and act as a keystone species for keeping the health of entire ecosystems in balance. While there is a good deal of

PASTAS AND RICE

If you are trying to incorporate more seafood into family meals but are faced with unenthusiastic eaters, pasta might be a good gateway. Given its role as comfort food in many of our families, pasta sets positive expectations for the dish before it even hits the table. Some of these recipes simply call for adding seafood to traditional and familiar preparations. Others are more intricate, though not prohibitively challenging. Because pasta is an inexpensive basis for a meal, it may allow you to budget in an extra seafood meal per week.

LOBSTER ROSSEJAT

SERVES 4

This Catalan dish (pronounced rose-ay-YACHT), which artfully combines rich shellfish, toasty pasta, and plenty of aioli, is my favorite recipe in this entire book. It is easy and so unique—a perfect recipe for entertaining. The noodles are toasted and then simmered in the lobster cooking liquid before a quick turn under the broiler. Under that final blast of heat, the tips of the noodles curl up and char slightly, adding a pleasant bitterness and crisp texture to the dish.

1 pound spaghetti

2 tablespoons extra-virgin olive oil, divided use

Salt

6 cups water

2 (1½-pound) lobsters (preferably new shell)

1 bay leaf

2 cloves garlic, thinly sliced

1 tablespoon smoked sweet paprika

1 recipe Classic Aioli (see page 257)

1 bunch fresh herbs, such as chervil or parsley, leaves only

Lemon wedges

Preheat the oven to 325°F.

Working in small batches, break the spaghetti into roughly 1-inch pieces and place on a baking sheet. Drizzle with 1½ teaspoons olive oil and toss to coat. Bake the noodles, tossing every few minutes, until deep brown all over, 10 to 12 minutes. (Keep a close eye on them as they can go from pale to overdone in no time.) Remove them from the oven and let them cool. If the pasta has cooked a little too much, scrape it onto a cool baking sheet to stop the cooking.

Bring 6 cups lightly salted water to a boil. Add the lobsters and bay leaf and cook for 6 minutes. Remove from the heat, transfer the lobsters to a bowl, and reserve the cooking water. Working over the bowl in order to catch all the juices, remove the meat from the lobsters and place it in a separate bowl. Add the shells (discarding the remaining innards) to the cooking water. Pour the lobster juices through a fine-mesh strainer into the cooking water. Bring to a gentle simmer to further infuse this quick broth.

Preheat the broiler to high.

Heat the remaining olive oil in a large paella or wide enameled pan over medium heat. Add the garlic and cook until the edges begin to brown. Add the paprika and cook, stirring, for 30 seconds. Add the noodles and toss to coat with the oil. Add two cups of the hot lobster broth and bring to an energetic simmer. Do not stir the noodles as they cook. When the broth has been absorbed, add another 2 cups, cooking until absorbed. Add the remaining broth and bring to a full boil. Immediately place the entire pan directly under the broiler. Cook until the noodles have absorbed almost all of the broth, 8 to 10 minutes. The noodles will curl up, and the ends will become crisp.

Remove the pan from the heat and set it aside while you cut the lobster tails into small medallions and the claws in half. Place the meat in neat arrangements around the pan. Place a very large dollop of aioli in the center of the dish and scatter the herbs over the top. Serve with the extra aioli and lemon wedges on the side.

SMOKED FISH MAC AND CHEESE

SERVES 4

Just about any variety of smoked seafood will shine in this recipe. I call for smoked trout, but you could easily substitute hot smoked salmon, whitefish, bluefish, canned smoked mackerel or sardines, or any kind of smoked shellfish. Whether you smoke it yourself or pop it straight out of a can, simply add the seafood at the very end of cooking so that the heat of the pasta and sauce gently warms the fish through. Take care when folding the seafood into the dish so you don't break up the pieces. I love to eat this drowned in Chile Vinegar Hot Sauce (page 250)—that tang and spice offers a welcome foil to all this savory richness.

1 pound macaroni

5 tablespoons butter

5 tablespoons flour

1 teaspoon ground mace

2 cups milk

Salt

8 ounces sharp white Cheddar, shredded

12 ounces smoked trout fillets, skinned and flaked

Cook the pasta in a large pot of boiling salted water, according to the package instructions, but drain the noodles 2 minutes before the end of the suggested cooking time, reserving ½ cup of the cooking water. Set aside.

Heat the butter in a small saucepan over medium heat until it begins to foam. Add the flour and cook, whisking constantly until smooth and a light roux forms, about 6 minutes. Reduce the heat to medium and continue to cook the roux, stirring regularly, until it is a deep caramel color. Stir in the mace and cook until lightly toasted, about 30 seconds. Add the milk and the reserved pasta cooking water, whisking constantly to incorporate and to break up any lumps. Reduce the heat to medium-low and simmer, stirring constantly, until the sauce has thickened and coats the back of a wooden spoon, about 10 minutes. Season to taste with salt. Remove from heat and add the shredded cheddar, stirring to combine.

Preheat the broiler to medium.

Pour two-thirds of the cheese sauce over the cooked macaroni and stir until evenly coated. Add the flaked trout to the remaining cheese sauce, taking care not to break up or mash the delicate fish. Using a spatula, gently fold the fish mixture into the pasta. Spread the mac and cheese into an ovenproof casserole dish.

Broil the mac and cheese until the top is crisped and golden brown, with some charred tips, 10 to 12 minutes. Remove from the oven and serve immediately.

PASTA CRABONARA

SERVES 4

That's not a typo! This recipe breaks from tradition, substituting sweet crab for smoky bacon, but the result is just as creamy and satisfying as ever.

1 pound linguine

Salt

1 cup white wine

2 sprigs fresh thyme

2 strips lemon zest

2 teaspoons freshly ground pepper-allspice

2 cups half and half

4 large egg yolks

2 tablespoons chopped flat-leaf parsley

2 tablespoons chopped tarragon or chervil

1 pound crab meat, picked

Cook the linguine in a large pot of boiling salted water to al dente, according to the package instructions. Drain the pasta, reserving ¼ cup of the cooking water for the sauce.

In the same pot, combine the wine, thyme, lemon zest, and pepper-allspice, and bring to a boil. Cook until the smell of alcohol has dissipated, about 3 minutes. Add the half and half, and simmer for 5 minutes.

Meanwhile, whisk together the egg yolks in a small bowl. While whisking, slowly add a ladleful of the simmering sauce to temper the yolks. Reduce the heat to low, add the yolk mixture to the sauce, and cook, stirring continuously, until it begins to thicken, about 5 minutes. Add the chopped parsley and tarragon, crab meat, and reserved pasta cooking water. Check the seasoning and adjust if needed. Bring the sauce to a simmer, add the pasta, and cook until the sauce is thickened and the pasta well coated, 4 to 5 minutes. Serve immediately.

LINGUINE WITH CANNED SHRIMP AND BUTTER

SERVES 4

This is my wife's favorite easy weeknight meal—after cooking the pasta, the sauce takes less than 5 minutes to come together. It's a great way to keep seafood in your weekly meal plan even if dropping by the store for the catch of the day isn't possible.

1 pound linguine

4 tablespoons butter, divided use

2 cloves garlic, thinly sliced

4 tablespoons chopped flat-leaf parsley or chives

2 (4-ounce) cans Oregon or Maine shrimp, drained and liquid reserved

Salt

Freshly ground pepper-allspice (optional)

Cook the linguine in a large pot of boiling salted water to al dente, according to the package instructions. Drain the pasta, reserving ½ cup of the cooking water for the sauce.

Heat 2 tablespoons of the butter in a large sauté pan over medium heat. Add the garlic and cook until just barely colored, about 3 minutes. Add the reserved shrimp liquid and the reserved pasta cooking water and bring to a boil. Add the cooked pasta and parsley and cook until heated through. Stir in the shrimp and the remaining 2 tablespoons of butter, then toss to combine and melt the butter. Check for seasoning and adjust if necessary. Serve with freshly ground pepper-allspice over the top, if desired.

SEAFOOD RISOTTO

SERVES 4

Almost any seafood can be used for this dish—consider a mix of small bay scallops, pieces of swordfish marinated with vinegar, canned smoked seafood (clams, mussels, oysters, salmon, sardines), or chunks of meaty mahi, wahoo, or tilefish. Whatever your choice, cut it into bite-size pieces so that it cooks evenly and stir gently so as not to crush the meat to bits.

5 tablespoons butter, divided use

3 tablespoons extra-virgin olive oil

1 large fennel bulb, diced

2 cloves garlic, sliced

1½ cups Arborio or carnaroli rice

2 cups white wine

4 cups hot stock, such as Basic Fish Stock (page 93), Shellfish Stock (page 96), or Seagreen Stock (page 95)

Salt

1½ pounds seafood, cut into bite-size pieces

2 tablespoons chopped flat-leaf parsley

2 tablespoons chopped tarragon or chives

Heat 3 tablespoons of the butter and the olive oil in a large, heavy pot over medium heat. Add the fennel and garlic and cook until translucent, about 7 minutes. Add the rice and cook, stirring frequently, until it begins to take on a toasty aroma, 8 to 10 minutes. Add the white wine, increase the heat to high, and cook, stirring constantly, until the alcohol smell has dissipated. Season the hot stock with salt, then add 2 cups of the stock to the rice, stirring every 30 seconds. Reduce the heat to medium and cook until the stock is almost fully absorbed. Add the remaining stock and continue to cook, stirring less frequently. When about half of the stock is absorbed, add the seafood and stir once to combine. Turn off the heat, cover the pan, and let sit until the seafood has cooked through, about 5 minutes. Add the remaining 2 tablespoons of butter and the chopped parsley and tarragon, stirring gently to combine. Serve immediately.

SEAFOOD PAELLA

SERVES 4

A good paella starts with a great stock. Taking the time to make a really rich, deeply flavorful stock will repay you with a paella that will have your friends talking for days. Any of the stocks in this book will work well (see pages 92 to 96). I suggest making double or triple batch of stock—it freezes well, which makes hosting another paella party a cinch to pull off.

6 tablespoons extra virgin olive oil, divided use

1 small onion, finely diced

1 red bell pepper, stemmed, seeded, and finely diced

3 cloves garlic, thinly sliced

2 tablespoons tomato paste

1 tablespoon smoked sweet paprika

10 saffron threads

6 cups Basic Fish Stock (page 93) or Shellfish Stock (page 96)

Salt

1 pound meaty white fish, such as Pacific rockfish, cobia, striped bass, weakfish, or sturgeon, cut into 1-inch cubes

½ pound squid, cut into small rings

12 littleneck clams or ½ pound shrimp, head on if possible

1½ cups Arborio or Valencia rice

½ cup frozen green peas

Classic Aioli (page 257)

Heat 4 tablespoons of the olive oil in a large pot over medium heat. Add the onion, pepper, and garlic, and cook for 2 minutes. Add the tomato paste, increase the heat to high, and cook until the paste is a shade darker, about 5 minutes. Add the paprika and saffron and cook, stirring, for 1 minute. Add the stock, season with salt, and simmer for 10 minutes. Reduce the heat to low. Add the white fish, squid, and clams, and cook for 5 minutes. Carefully drain the mixture, reserving the stock and the seafood and vegetable mixture separately.

Preheat the oven to 350°F.

Heat the remaining 2 tablespoons of olive oil in a large paella pan or wide enameled pan over medium heat. Add the rice and cook until it is opaque, about 5 minutes. Add the reserved stock, bring to a boil, and cook until about two-thirds of the broth has been absorbed. Turn off the heat. Scatter the peas over the rice and arrange the reserved seafood and vegetables over the top.

Place the pan in the oven and bake until the remaining broth has been absorbed, about 10 minutes. At this point, the dish can be served as is, or the pan can be placed back on the stove over medium heat for about 5 minutes to crisp the bottom layer of rice. Serve with aioli on the side.

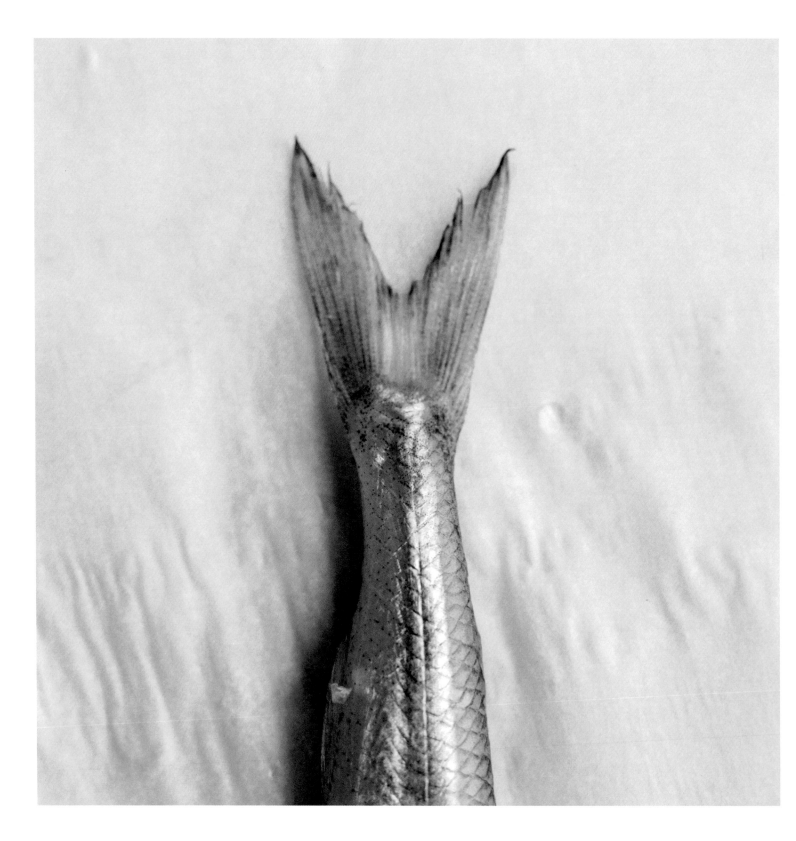

FISH SPECIES BY FLAVOR PROFILE, CATEGORY, AND COOKING METHODS

There are plenty of fish in the sea. While the verity of this old idiom is challenged by our unsustainable fishing practices, it still holds true in terms of culinary opportunity. As diners we tend not stray far from our few favorite fish, namely shrimp, salmon, and tuna. While not entirely to blame for the depletion of our ocean stocks, our particular preferences place a great burden on just a few species while other equally or more delicious fish languish at the market. So venture out of the shallows. Ask for something a little different and have fun exploring new tastes. Yes, indeed, there are plenty of fish in the sea. And none of them are scary.

Flaky White Fish

These fish all share a similar size and texture of flake. Their flavor is generally quite mild, ranging from the blank canvas of tilapia to the savory, cool flavor of cod and halibut.

CATFISH: The many market varieties of catfish all have similar eating characteristics. Flavors range from sweet and clean to slightly muddy. I'm particularly fond of fish harvested from brackish or saltwaters. *fry, roast, sauté, stew*

CHEEKS: This cut from the head of the fish, most often available from the cod family, skate, halibut, and monkfish, are all cooked the same way. They render a very gelatinous sauce when sautéed with butter or olive oil, parsley, and sherry. They also are fantastic added to stews. *sauté, stew*

COD: Both Atlantic and Pacific cod cook in much the same way. It is a meaty, white-fleshed fish with a large flake. *fry, poach, roast, salted, sauté, steam, stew*

DOGFISH, SPINY: This small shark has a firm, monkfish-like texture, though it flakes delicately. Very sweet, briny flavor. *broil, fry, grill, roast, sauté, smoke, stew*

HADDOCK: This staple of northern cuisine, especially in Maine, is very similar to cod, with a mild taste, firm texture, and small, dense flake. *broil, fry, roast, sauté, smoke, stew*

HAKE: This northern fish, a relative of cod, has a very sweet flavor, mild brininess, and a very small flake that requires delicate cooking. *broil, roast, sauté, steam*

HALIBUT: The largest of the flatfish, this snow-white-fleshed fish is often very large in size, with a pleasantly mild, blank canvas–like flavor. *fry, poach, roast, sauté, stew*

POLLOCK, ALASKAN: This is the most common whitefish variety found in many packaged products, such as fish sticks and breaded fillets. Its clean mild flavor is a great canvas for many flavors, though it can be overpowered by too strong of a pairing. It has a benchmark flaky texture with a sweet, moderate flavor. *broil, fry, sauté, stew*

POLLOCK, ATLANTIC: This is the firmest textured northern whitefish with the most assertive flavor. The light, pinkish-gray fillets have great integrity of texture, a toothsome bite, and a briny sweet finish. *broil, sauté, smoke, stew*

SABLEFISH: This incredibly svelte queen of the northern Pacific is about as elegant as seafood gets. It's also known as black cod though its silken texture has led to the unofficial nickname butterfish, which describes its character rather well. An elastic texture when raw yields to a beautiful flake. A mild but broad flavor pairs well with acidic ingredients and herbs. *broil, fry, poach, roast, sauté, smoke*

TILAPIA: Best used as a gateway fish, tilapia has a very mild flavor and toothsome texture that make it a good canvas for the ingredients it's paired with. It is very lean and is always sold skin off. *fry, poach, roast, sauté, stew*

WHITING: Very similar to hake in its fine texture and very small flake (though not as sweet), whiting pairs very well with smoke and acidic flavors. Best cooked with the skin on, though removed before serving. *broil, poach, sauté, smoke, steam*

FLAT FISH

While the fish in this category, with their very small flake and delicate structure, differ from cod-like fish greatly in terms of texture, the flavors are all similar. They perform well in similar preparations.

DAB: This small flatfish has characteristics of sole: a delicate texture, small flake, and sweet taste. It is best prepared whole. *broil, fry, grill*

FLOUNDER: This group encompasses a large variety of species, all with very similar culinary characteristics. The mild-flavored, thin white to off-grey fillets are best served with the skin off. *fry, poach, fillet, steam*

HALIBUT: Though halibut is a flatfish, due to its large size, it cooks more like a flaky white fish (see above). *fry, poach, roast, sauté, stew*

SOLE: The most delicate of the flatfish, sole is very similar to flounder, with which it is interchangeable. Its smooth, delicate white meat has a mild and elegant flavor. *fry, poach, fillet, steam*

Round Fish

These are the fish that we tend to think of as **fillet fish**, or pan fish. Their texture is more taut than that of the flaky white and flat fishes due to their increased activity levels. Often these are cooked and served with their skin on. The texture of many of these fish are similar, so I break them out by depth of flavor.

MEDIUM-FLAVORED FILLET FISH

BLACK BASS: A nice fish for whole presentations, black bass has an exceptionally elegant flavor and a thin-skinned fillet. *poach, sauté, steam*

BLUEGILL: This freshwater species, commonly caught as a game fish, has a delightfully sweet flavor and firm texture. *fry, sauté*

BUTTERFISH: These small silver fish have very cute fillets usually no more than 4 inches long. It's very hard to remove the skin without taking too much of the fillet, but luckily the skin eats very well. Most often served pan-dressed (head and fins removed). *fry, grilled, sauté*

CROAKER: These relatively small fish have a mild, sweet flavor, thin skin, and a slightly elastic bite. They can either be pan-dressed or filleted. *fry, sauté*

DRUM, BLACK: This cousin to the Red Drum (Redfish) is a wonderful eating fish. The textured flake is snappy and slightly meaty and carries a moderate but clean, briny flavor. *broil, fry, grill, sauté, stew*

DRUM, RED: Also commonly known as redfish, made exceedingly popular in Cajun cuisine by the legendary Paul Prudhomme. Popularly presented under a thick layer of blackening spice, the fillet actually has a quite delicate flavor that is worth coaxing out with milder accompaniments such as fresh herbs. *broil, fry, grill, sauté, stew*

GRUNTS: Once very common in southern cuisine, grunts have small, pan-size fillets, moderate flavor, and a medium-firm texture. "Grits and grunts" once described a common culinary use of them. *fry, poach, sauté*

JOHN DORY: This very unique-looking fish is not commonly available in markets. Always served in fillet form, it is distinguished by having three separate pieces to each fillet that naturally separate when cooking. It has a moderate, sweet flavor; good briny finish; and firm yet smooth texture. *broil, poach, sauté, stew*

MULLET: People don't think fish anymore when they hear *mullet*, even though that's where the awesome 80s haircut got its name. Once a very common food fish, it has a perfectly dense texture with a medium flake, with a soft yet charismatic flavor. *broil, fry, sauté, smoke, stew*

PERCH: These small pan-sized fish, frequently caught in the Great Lakes and the Chesapeake, though commonly distributed, have a very mild flavor, thin skin, and a delicate texture that can be served pan dressed. *broil, fry, sauté*

PIKE: This freshwater game fish is popular in European cuisine and in the United States, especially in the Midwestern states. Fillets have a delicate, small flake but good structural integrity, a snappy bite, and a moderate but charismatic flavor. *broil, fry, sauté, smoke*

POMPANO: A matte silver fish with a very thick skin, pompano has a fine-grained meaty texture with a small flake. Its flavor is very buttery, with a sweet, mild aftertaste. *broil, grill, smoke, stew*

PORGY: This category, which includes scup and sheepshead, has snapper-like qualities. These medium flavored, flaky, sweet fish are thin-skinned and great for fillet or whole preparations. *fry, grill, roast, sauté, broil, stew*

REDFISH, ACADIAN: This deep-water northern species, also known as ocean perch, has beautiful pinkish-red skin, mild to moderate flavor, a lean fillet, and snapper-like qualities. *fry, sauté, stew*

ROCKFISH, PACIFIC: There are dozens of species that fall into this category; many are commonly referred to as rock cod. They generally share a few common characteristics: a dense yet flaky structure and a moderate, briny flavor that plays well with most other ingredients. Great for kebabs. *broil, grill, roast, sauté, stew*

SCUP: *See* Porgy.

SHEEPSHEAD: *See* Porgy.

SKATE: Skate, like sharks, don't have bones but a skeletal structure of cartilage. Wholly unique in its texture, skate's ribbons of flesh are delicately strung together in a fan-like shape. Its flavor is very sweet with a hint of brine. It is best cooked and served on the cartilage. *broil, fry, poach, roast, sauté, stew*

TAUTOG: Also known as blackfish, this deep-water species has a unique sweetness with a texture similar to grouper, for which it is a great stand-in. The skin has a seam of scales running down its lateral line that are very hard to remove, so I like to cook this fish with its skin on, but remove it before serving. *broil, fry, grill, sauté, stew*

TRIGGERFISH: This dense fish is a textural cross between snapper and grouper with meaty fillets, a mild sweetness, and a briny finish. *broil, fry, grill, sauté, smoke, stew*

TRIPLETAIL: Very similar to grouper, this fish has dense but flaky flesh and broad, mild, yet charismatic flavors. *broil, grill, sauté, stew*

FULL-FLAVORED FILLET FISH

BLUEFISH: This fish is mild when small and fuller-flavored when larger. The bloodline—the highly flavored, dark-colored flesh just under the skin—can easily be removed after cooking. *broil, grill, roast, sauté, smoke*

GROUPER: Encompassing many species, these fish all have charismatic flavor and meaty fillets, ranging from hand size to far larger. It is a staple of Southern cuisine and is highly regarded for its firm texture. *fry, grill, roast, sauté*

MACKEREL, BOSTON: These sleek, bullet-shaped fish yield small, smooth, fine-grained fillets. They are highly flavored and best served with the skin on, as the meat can fall apart. *broil, fry, pickle, sauté, smoke*

MACKEREL, SPANISH: This gorgeous silver fish with yellow spots has varying flavors, depending on where it comes from. Fish caught in northern regions can have very clean, bright flavors. A more southerly catch tends to be larger and have a finer texture and slightly more robust flavor. *broil, pickle, fry, grill, sauté, smoke, stew*

SHAD/ROE: This cult favorite floods into eastern shores every spring. It's a bony, difficult-to-cut fish that is worth the effort as the reddish-gray meat has a delicate character with a mild brininess. Fortunately, it is most often sold already filleted. Its roe, prepared separately, is a delicacy and, like shad fillets, tastes best sautéed in butter. *sauté*

SNAPPERS: These universally loved fish, which include many different kinds, such as red, lane, mutton, vermillion, and so on, all share a beautiful, elegant flavor. Small and firm with a delicate flake and a thin skin, all of these fish pair well with a wide range of seasonings. Though snapper is most common in Southern cuisine, you will find it in stores and on menus almost everywhere. *fry, poach, sauté, steam, stew*

TILEFISH: This opaque, pinkish-white fish is akin to mahi and striped bass in texture. Its very large flake gives it a more steak-like texture. It has a firm but sweet flavor, though I find that it shows best when paired with a rich sauce or accompaniment to counteract the somewhat prevalent tinny flavor. *grill, poach, sauté, stew*

WEAKFISH AND SPOTTED SEA TROUT: These two distinct fish are commonly used interchangeably as they have very similar culinary characteristics. Both are highly prized for their briny, sweet flesh, which is delicately textured and rich. *broil, grill, sauté, smoke*

WRECKFISH: Though not caught in large quantities, this southern Atlantic species is famed for its great strength and finesse of flavor, density of texture, and culinary potential. It works well when paired with sweet-sour ingredients, such as citrus fruit like grapefruit. *grill, poach, roast, sauté, smoke, stew*

YELLOWTAIL: This relative of the jack family, also known as hiramasa or seriola, has an incredibly rich, luxurious fillet. This is a fabulous fish for serving raw (see notes on serving raw fish, page 32). Because its defining characteristic is its richness, it's best suited to cooking methods in which some of the fat is allowed to cook out, self-basting the fish. *broil, grill, sauté, smoke*

Meaty Dense Fish

This group includes fish that require long slow cooking times due to a high amount of connective tissue or a very dense texture.

AMBERJACK: These fillets have a pleasantly chewy texture with a briny and aromatic flavor similar to grouper. *grill, sauté, broil*

COBIA: Also known as lemonfish, this is a firm, flaky, grayish-white fillet. It has a moderate flavor and is usually served with the skin off. *broil, fry, grill, roast, sauté, stew*

MONKFISH: This fish is charming in its ugliness. Most often sold in loins, of which there are two per fish, it can also come to market in the form of tail, with a thin purplish skin and a single cartilaginous spine running down its center. It has a very snappy, elastic texture with meat-like density and chew. Loins can be sliced into medallions or, when small, cooked whole as a single portion. When served on the bone it can mimic meat in the form of an osso buco, and the bone lends great richness and structure to any liquid in which it's cooked. *broil, pickle (cook first), fry, roast, sauté, stew*

SEA ROBIN: Not a common food fish in the United States (though I wish it were), these small ground fish have a monkfish-like texture. The small loins are almost always served on the bone, which adds richness to any liquid it's cooked in. *sauté, stew*

STRIPED BASS: Also known as rockfish on the East Coast, this "King of Fish" has a very dense, meaty flesh and a very clean yet robust flavor. It's one of the few fish that really benefits from a crisp skin and hard sear. Due to their active nature, these fish have a lot of highly developed muscle tissue, which breaks down in high-heat cooking but makes them unsuitable for methods such as poaching or slow roasting. *broil, grill, sauté*

STURGEON, FARMED: Once plentiful in the wild, this species is enjoying a culinary resurgence due to successful farming operations. It has very dense meat streaked with thick bands of fat and a texture similar to swordfish. It is as good for kebabs as it is in scaloppini preparations. *fry, pickled (cook first), grill, sauté, broil, stew, smoke*

Small Silver Fish

This super healthful category includes a host of species that are rich in flavor and high in omega-3s. Many of these are served either whole or filleted; the tiny bones are usually edible or easy enough to pull out.

ANCHOVIES, FRESH: These small, very mild fish are sometimes cooked whole with the head on, or are otherwise headed and gutted. *broil, pickle, fry, grill, sauté, smoke*

ANCHOVIES, SALTED/PICKLED: Pickled anchovies are often labeled boquerones and are mild flavored with a whitish-gray color. The salted variety, aged six months or more before canning, have a fuller and more complex flavor. Great as part of a fritto misto. *fry, as is*

EULACHON: Also known as candlefish, this small, very fatty fish is served much like sardines, anchovies, or smelts—whole or headed and gutted. They are delightful when lightly smoked prior to cooking. *broil, pickle, fry, grill, sauté, smoke*

HERRING: These small fish offer very dynamic culinary possibilities. With their high fat content, they can range from mild and clean in taste to very full-flavored when coaxed. They can be filleted or prepared whole. *broil, pickle, fry, grill, sauté, smoke*

SARDINES: Often sold as herring (which they resemble), these small fish offer plenty of culinary possibilities. They can be be filleted or prepared whole and, depending on the seasoning, range from very full-flavored to very mild and clean, despite their high fat content. *broil, pickle, fry, grill, sauté, smoke*

SMELT: These small silverside fish are commonly sold dressed and frozen, though they can be found fresh in the early spring. They have a wonderful, delicate flavor. Smelts are always served on the bone, which are very small and delicate and wholly edible. *broil, fry, grill, sauté, smoke*

Orange-Fleshed Fish

Think of this as the salmon category. Almost all salmon species (wild and farmed), trout, and char are interchangeable in most recipes and preparations.

NOTE: *Though trout is often not orange fleshed (it sometimes is), it fits into this category in culinary application.*

ARCTIC CHAR: This is a pale orange-fleshed fish with a delightfully yielding texture and slightly milder flavor than that of salmon. Sometimes referred to as "salmon lite." *broil, cure, grill, poach, sauté, smoke, roast*

SALMON, CHUM: Light in flavor, this wild salmon has a nuanced character. It is not as common as a food species as other salmons, due only to cultural preferences and the greater popularity of other wild salmons. Its character is quite appealing thanks to its balance of "salmon-ness" with a leaner fat content. *broiul, cure, grill, poach, roast, sauté, smoke, stew*

SALMON, COHO: My favorite of all the salmon varieties, this has the most structured flavor and easily pairs with a wide range of ingredients. On the lighter side of fatty, with a firm texture when cooked. *broil, cure, grill, poach, roast, sauté, smoke, stew*

SALMON, FARMED: This darling of the culinary world, due to its consistent availability and affable personality, is an easy fish to prepare. It's often considered a "gateway" fish since it is a great vehicle on which to learn common cooking methods that can be applied to lesser available species. There is a wide spectrum of quality in farmed salmon: Some are incredibly rich and flavorful, while others are leaner and milder in flavor. *broil, cure, grill, poach, roast, sauté, smoke, stew*

SALMON, KING: The richest and by far most expensive of all types of salmon. It has a very distinguished flavor and very high fat content and is worth every penny. *broil, cure, grill, poach, roast, sauté, smoke, stew*

SALMON, PINK: This salmon has the lightest color and mildest flavor of them all, as well as the leanest texture. It stands alone among orange fish, as it must be treated more delicately to account for its relatively lower fat content. Canned pink salmon, the most common way to find this fish, is great for fish cakes and pasta preparations. *broil, poach, roast, smoke, steam*

SALMON, SOCKEYE: This darkly hued red fillet has a delightful gamey/wild flavor. Its assertive nature allows for more robust flavor pairings and makes it a near perfect pairing with light red wines. *broil, cure, grill, poach, roast, sauté, smoke, stew*

TROUT: Often sold head-on and butterflied, these fish make for great stuffed preparations. The delicate and lean flesh benefits from cooking in its skin. Its broad flavor and lack of brininess pair very well with butter-based sauces that have a slight acidity. *broil, grill, sauté, smoke, roast*

TROUT, STEELHEAD: Similar to farmed salmon in appearance, steelhead has a slightly more angular and acute flavor and denser texture. It's best cooked with the skin on and removed before serving. *broil, grill, sauté, smoke*

Steak Fishes

These are the fish best suited to the grill or broiler. They are typically very large fish, such as swordfish, and so are never sold whole but rather cut into cross sections or steaks.

ALBACORE TUNA: This lean, light pink tuna has a very mild flavor. This fish can dry out easily, so I recommend cooking to a medium doneness. *fry, grill, poach, sauté, smoke, stew*

BONITO TUNA: This pale pink tuna has a very mild flavor and very lean textured flake, similar to albacore. This fish can dry out easily, so don't cook it beyond medium. *fry, grill, poach, sauté, smoke, stew*

MAHIMAHI: This one-of-a-kind fish is popular in Hawaiian and island cuisine. Often paired with fruit, this pinkish-white fillet is meaty, with a somewhat chicken-like texture. It has a very balanced flavor (though it can be somewhat tinny), with a balanced richness and briny sweet finish. Its thick skin must be removed before serving. *broil, grill, sauté*

SWORDFISH: With a rich, buttery, steak-like texture, this giant fish has a mild flavor despite its richness. The bloodline—the dark colored tissue coursing through the center—is more highly flavored and not to everyone's taste. It can be easily removed after cooking. Swordfish makes great kebabs. *broil, grill, roast, smoke, stew*

TUNA, FRESH (RED-FLESHED VARIETIES): There are a number of tunas that fall into this category. They range from the very, very rich, such as bluefin, all the way down to the very lean blackfin. The richer fish, so highly prized, have been subject to unsustainable fishing. The less popular, leaner types (skipjack and blackfin) can have a hint of iron to their flavor, but with the right pairing or rich sauce, you can coax a very gentle sweetness and big briny flavor from them. *broil, grill, poach, sauté, smoke, stew*

WAHOO: The largest member of the mackerel family, wahoo is a unique culinary experience. Much like tuna, its rich texture is defined by concentric rings. It is leaner but still very rich, with a smooth, creamy mouthfeel. Its flavor is not nearly as robust as tuna, but it cooks and presents in much the same way. *fry, grill, smoke, stew*

TECHNIQUES

Most people I know would like to cook seafood at home more often but are timid about doing so. Their most common fear? That cooking fish will leave a lingering "presence" about the house. Well, that problem is so very simple to solve. If it smells like fish, don't buy it! Fresh, fine-quality seafood should smell sweet, like cucumbers or ocean breezes. So find a good fish market and buy the freshest fish they have (which might not be the fish specified in the recipe you had in mind). With a great piece of fish in hand, you're 90 percent of the way to a great meal.

Most fish fall into just a few flavor and texture categories and are quite interchangeable, so be flexible and willing to try a different species. For instance, if you are comfortable cooking cod, then by all means you can cook pollock. The following recipes call for a specific fish for demonstration purposes, but know that any seafood recommended for that same technique can be substituted. And while the accompanying sauces are well suited to the particular preparation, feel free to mix and match as you like. Indeed, treat this section as a series of educational "how-tos" rather than hard and fast recipes. Take a read through the following techniques and familiarize yourself with the process before you begin. Then cook with confidence and, most importantly, have fun. If you can do that, then you are pretty much guaranteed to enjoy the meal.

ROAST

When cooking at home, slow roasting is the best method for preserving the succulence and texture for which pristine seafood is so admired. The key to roasting is maintaining an even, constant temperature. To me, slow roasting means cooking at 300°F or less; I prefer going as low as 275°F.

To prepare seafood for slow roasting, season it with salt, drizzle it with a little olive oil, and arrange it on a pan with a good amount of space between each fillet so they can cook evenly. Place the pan in the oven and check after about 15 minutes. At 275°F, the rule of thumb is 20 to 25 minutes of cooking for each inch of thickness (but most seafood is not that thick, so you need to check earlier). When done, the fish may not look much different than it did when it went in, but give the flesh a gentle squeeze between two fingers—it should flake apart. This guarantees it is fully cooked.

This test is especially important with salmon. With higher-heat methods, salmon's color generally changes from orange to light pink as it cooks. In the case of slow roasting, it mostly stays dark orange. With white fish such as halibut (another great candidate for slow roasting), the fish will go from translucent to opaque when fully cooked, giving a more obvious impression.

ROASTED SALMON WITH SEAWEED BUTTER

Best for Flaky White Fish and Orange-Fleshed Fish

Lightly oil an oven-safe pan. Arrange the fish skin side down in the pan and season generously with salt. Place the pan in 275°F oven.

Remove from the oven when just done, about 20 minutes per inch of thickness. The flesh will flake under gentle pressure.

Remove the skin by sliding a spatula between the flesh and skin and transfer the fish to a plate.

Dot the fish with thin slices of Seaweed Butter (see page 236). Let the butter melt to thoroughly coat the fish and serve.

SAUTÉ

When it comes to cooking protein, sautéing is the method that most likely comes to mind. The first rule of a good sauté is to leave the pan alone. We're used to watching dramatic cooking shows where flames (and tempers) run high, but honestly, you don't want either of those things in your kitchen. When cooking in a sauté pan, the only form of heat is through direct contact with the pan. The more you flip and turn, the less you are actually cooking. The benefit of sautéing is you can create a delicate, lightly seared flavor that heightens the seafood's original taste. (But too much of this sear can be detrimental.) Plus, you can make a sauce in the same pan, either to help complete the cooking or afterward, once the seafood has been removed. These pan sauces are wonderfully easy and require just a few ingredients.

When sautéing, you can spoon foaming, aromatic browned butter over the fish, a luxurious technique known as *poele*. The delicious toasted butter solids, scented with herbs and garlic, permeate the flesh, and the resulting dish is very balanced—its richness undercut by the slight bitterness of the browned butter. Plus, you gain a wonderfully crisp skin.

The Canadian Rule

I first came across the "Canadian Rule" in my favorite seafood book, *Blues* by John Hersey. Now, I'm not sure why it's called the Canadian Rule, or where in Canada it came from, or how long it's been around, but I do know that it generally works. As you get more practiced with seafood, you begin to develop an intuition about things and generally you can tell if something is done just by look, feel, sound. As a general guideline the Canadian Rule provides principle and some good structure to for your learning and that the rule states as follows: "Measure the fish at the thickest part, and then cook 10 minutes to the inch. It's amazing: this works pretty well with all kinds of fish and no matter how you are cooking, whether broiling, baking, poaching, frying, grilling, whatever." That said, the Canadian Rule doesn't tell you how hot your fire is, so this is just a guideline.

Best Pans

The original nonstick pan was the heavy, well-seasoned cast-iron skillet. Over the years, lighter nonstick pans have evolved, most of them lined with various coatings, some of which have turned out to be not so healthy for us. I've recently been turned on to ceramic-lined Zwilling® pans, which are hands down the best nonstick cookware I've ever worked with and are truly the easiest to maintain.

SAUTÉED CREOLE CATFISH

Best for Flaky White Fish, Mild to Medium, and Full Flavored Fillet Fish, Orange-Fleshed Fish

Slice the fish on a bias into ½-inch-thick pieces. Season one side generously with Creole Seasoning (page 253).

Heat peanut oil and butter over medium heat until the butter begins to bubble. Place lemon halves and fish, seasoned side down, into the hot pan.

Cook the fish on one side until the flesh is opaque almost all the way through, about 4 minutes. Turn fish and cook 1 minute more.

Remove from the heat, and serve, seasoned side up, with seared lemon over Fennel Coleslaw (see page 272).

POELE RED DRUM WITH VINAIGRETTE

Best for Mild to Medium or Full-Flavored Fillet Fish, Orange-Fleshed Fish, and Meaty, Dense Fish

Flip the fish and add 2 tablespoons of butter, 2 cloves of crushed garlic, and 2 sprigs of fresh thyme. (This quantity will work for 2 to 4 fillets, as it allows you to spoon the butter easily. Do not cook more than 4 fillets at a time.)

Cook, skin side up, for 3 minutes while continuously basting the fish with the melted butter. Remove the fish from the pan, allowing the excess fat to drip off.

Score fish as shown for Sautéed Black Drum (see page 178). Season the fillet with salt and pepper-allspice. Heat the pan over high heat and add 1 tablespoon of peanut oil. When the oil is almost smoking, add the fish, skin side down, gently pressing the fillets to prevent curling and ensure even cooking. Cook until it begins to crisp, 5 to 7 minutes.

Plate the fish and top with the crisped thyme and garlic pieces. Spoon Vinaigrette (see page 239) around the fish.

SAUTÉED BLACK DRUM WITH BLACK BUTTER SAUCE AND RICE PILAF

Best for Mild to Medium and Full-Flavored Fillet Fish, Orange-Fleshed Fish

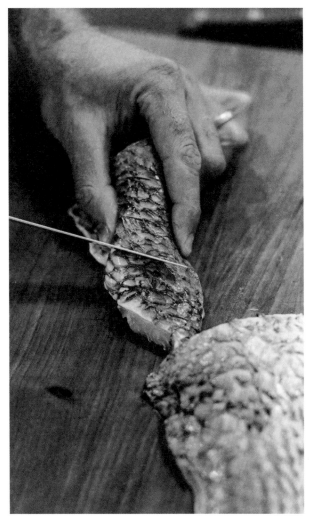

Score the skin, taking care not to cut into the flesh.

Heat butter over high heat until it just begins to brown. Add a dash of peanut oil. Season the flesh side of the fish with salt.

Add fish to the hot pan, skin side down. Gently press the fillets into the pan to prevent curling and ensure even cooking. Reduce heat to medium and sear until skin begins to crisp, 5 to 7 minutes.

Flip the fish and cook 2 minutes more before removing from pan.

In the same pan, prepare the Black Butter Sauce (page 250)

Plate the fish over Rice Pilaf with Almonds and Fennel (see page 288). Spoon the sauce onto the plate.

GRIDDLE

Griddling is very similar to sautéing, but it uses less fat and can be served right in the pan. There are a number of beautiful cast iron griddles available—the key is to use a flat one, not a ridged grill pan. One of the advantages of griddling is that the super-high heat turns marinades into a crust that adheres to the ingredient, thus giving texture and flavor.

HEAD-ON SHRIMP WITH SALMORIGLIO
Best for Shellfish, Squid, and Meaty, Dense Fish

Very lightly oil the griddle and heat over high heat. Place the shrimp on the smoking hot griddle and cook, undisturbed, until they begin to turn color about halfway up the side, about 6 minutes. The shrimp used here are U-12 size. Adjust the cooking time for smaller or larger shrimp.

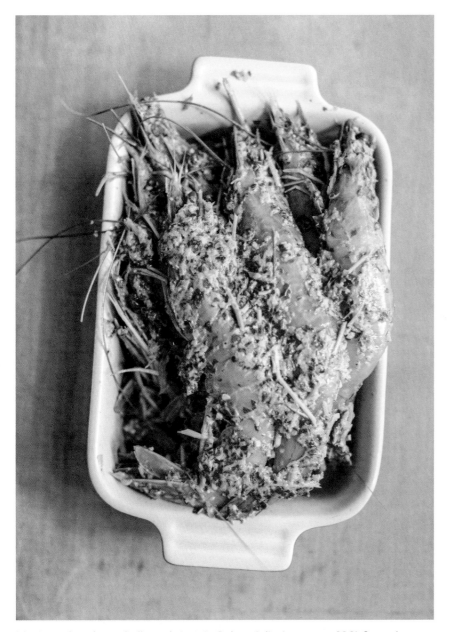

Marinate head-on, shell-on shrimp in Salmoriglio (see page 230) for at least 20 minutes and up to overnight.

When the shrimp are cooked halfway through and becoming opaque, flip them and turn off the heat. Allow the shrimp to sit until cooked through, at least 2 minutes more. Serve the shrimp on the sizzling griddle.

PAN ROAST

While I don't believe it's appropriate to deeply caramelize a fish's flesh, a slight singe to the skin can be quite pleasant, especially in fattier fish. Starting the fish skin-side down in a super hot pan then finishing it in a low oven will continue to crisp the skin while allowing for an even, smooth cooking process for the fillet.

This method works well for just a few fish, notably those with a rich texture that will retain their moist, luxurious mouthfeel in contrast to the crisp skin. My favorite species for this are trout, sablefish, salmon, bluefish, and mackerel.

PAN-ROASTED TROUT WITH SKORDALIA

Best for Orange-Fleshed Fish, Full-Flavored Fillet Fish

This recipe uses herbs to retain moisture and add flavor to the fish. Ask your fishmonger to butterfly the fish for you for ease of preparation and elegance in serving.

Heat the pan over high heat and add a small amount of peanut oil. Season the outside of the trout generously with salt.

Arrange the fish in the pan; if using fillets, place them skin side down. Cook for 2 to 3 minutes over high heat. The skin will crackle and crisp. Cover the top of the fish with herbs such as basil.

Cover the dish. (This will capture the heat so it will cook evenly while still crisping the skin.) Place the dish in a 300°F oven for 12 to 15 minutes per pound. Remove from the oven and serve whole with Skordalia (see page 240).

BROIL

Broiling is essentially a cross between grilling and roasting—you are applying extreme heat to one side while using the ambient temperature of the oven to cook the seafood through. I usually use a broiler to finish a roasting process. When pan-roasting, one browns the meat before transferring it to the oven. With broiling, you reverse that process and brown the dish throughout the cooking time. This is especially useful in dishes like deviled crab or oysters Rockefeller, recipes that take just a few minutes to cook all the way through but benefit from the deep charred flavor that can only be achieved by the high heat of the broiler.

BROILED SWORDFISH

Best for Steak Fishes, Orange-Fleshed Fish, Full-Flavored Fillet Fish

Season swordfish with salt and pepper-allspice. For every 12 ounces of fish, mash together 2 tablespoons of softened butter, 1 minced shallot, 1 sliced clove garlic, and the juice of ½ lemon. Spread over the top of the fish.

Sprinkle the fish with Pernod.

Place the seasoned fish on a lightly oiled ovenproof pan. Place on the highest rack of the broiler set to high.

Cook for 10 minutes for each inch of thickness. (See the Canadian Rule, page 175.) Remove from the oven and serve.

POACH

Both delicate and more robustly flavored varieties of seafood benefit from poaching. There are two ways to poach. With shallow poaching, seafood is partially submerged in a gently flavored broth, known as *cuisson* in French cooking, which is then reduced and used as sauce. (Keep the seafood warm in a very low oven while you finish the sauce.) Shallow poached seafood benefits from being served alongside other components that maintain a lot of heat, such as risotto, pilaf, or lentil stew.

Deep-poach cooking requires seafood to be fully submerged in a very flavorful liquid. An accompanying sauce is made separately. Deep poaching seafood, especially if chilled in the broth to fully develop the flavor before serving, is a great way to prepare a dish for serving chilled or at room temperature.

While the liquid for shallow poaching should be lightly seasoned with salt, since it will be reduced, deep poaching calls for an aggressively seasoned liquid. No matter the cooking style, lightly season the seafood about 5 minutes before cooking to firm the fillets. Though it is not customary to serve poached seafood with the skin on, it adds complexity and richness to the broth, especially when using the shallow method. The skin can be easily removed after cooking. Poaching should be done between 165°F and 180°F, preferably on the lower side.

SHALLOW-POACHED MACKEREL FILLET WITH PAN SAUCE

Best of Full-Flavored Fillet Fish, Flaky White-Fleshed Fish, Thinner Orange-Fleshed Fish

Make a broth of finely diced carrot, shallot, thyme, lemon peel, clove, and equal parts white or red wine and water. You should have just enough to cover your fish. Bring the liquid to 180°F. Season the fish lightly with salt.

Reduce the heat to low and add the fish to the broth, maintaining the temperature between 165°F and 175°F. Gently poach the fish until cooked through. Cook about 5 minutes for every ½ inch of thickness.

Transfer the fish to a warm plate. Remove the thyme, lemon peel, and clove; discard.

Continue to simmer the sauce until reduced to 2 tablespoons per serving. For each serving, whisk in ½ diced tomato and 1 tablespoon butter. Simmer the sauce until the butter is incorporated and season with chives. For a quick version of this sauce, see Buttery Seafood Essence (page 259).

Plate the mackerel and spoon the sauce over the fillet. Serve immediately.

DEEP-POACHED HALIBUT WITH GREEN GODDESS DRESSING

Best for Flaky White-Fleshed Fish, Orange-Fleshed Fish, or Shellfish

Remove the fish from the cooking liquid. If the skin has been left on, gently remove it by using a fish spatula. Discard the skin.

Combine 1 part red or white wine, 1 part red or white wine vinegar, 3 parts water, fresh thyme sprigs, garlic cloves, orange zest, juniper berries, and a bay leaf in a large pot. Season with salt. Heat over medium-high heat until 180°F. Season the fish lightly with salt on all sides and add to the poaching liquid. Reduce the heat to low. Use a thermometer to maintain the heat between 165°F and 175°F. Cook for 10 to 12 minutes per inch of thickness.

Spread Green Goddess Dressing (page 263) on a plate. Make a salad of ½ apple, shaved; ½ bulb of fennel, shaved; 2 sliced radishes; and 2 tablespoons of torn parsley leaves. Arrange the salad on the plate. Place the fish atop the sauce and salad.

STEAM

Steaming is a way to incorporate very nuanced flavors into delicate seafood, such as sole and black bass, and even more highly flavored seafood like herring, while keeping the cooking times very short. Adding aromatics to the steaming liquid gently perfumes both it and the seafood. The liquid itself can be wine (my preference) or stock, though water works perfectly well. Asian flavorings—cilantro, ginger, lemon grass, soy—take very well to steaming as they don't require lengthy cooking to meld their flavors and come into focus very quickly.

Seaweeds are a natural pairing when it comes to steaming and add a mildly sweet brininess to the fish. Try dried seaweed like nori or fresh such as rockweed, which is commonly sold with live lobsters. Fennel stalks can be used as a raft to elevate the fish above the liquid, while imparting their own beguiling flavor. Soy adds a potent yet nuanced backbone, while ginger, lemon grass, and citrus peel all provide a fresh, acidic punctuation. Richer spices such as bay leaf, cinnamon, and coriander seeds add real complexity.

STEAMED SHEEPSHEAD WITH CHILE OIL

Best for Mild to Medium-Flavored Fillet Fish, White-Fleshed Fish, Orange-Fleshed Fish

In a large pot, combine a cinnamon stick, an orange slice, fennel stalks, and rockweed, forming a raft on which the seafood will rest.

Place seasoned fish fillets on top of the aromatics. Add equal parts of white wine and water, no more than ½-inch deep. Bring to a simmer and cover. Cook until the fish is firm and cooked through, about 7 minutes per ½ inch of thickness.

Transfer the fish to a plate and serve drizzled with Chile Oil (see page 223).

FRY

When deep-frying, foods are breaded and then submerged in hot fat to cook until the exterior is crisped and browned. Vegetable oils that have high smoking points, such as soy or peanut, work best for frying. (Avoid olive oil, which has a lower smoking point.) Batters can range from heavy beer batters to light tempura-style ones, and breadings run the gamut from cornmeal to panko.

When choosing (or making) bread crumbs, it's important that no crust remains on the bread. The crust is already browned and will only cook further (or burn) in the fryer. The most popular breadcrumb for frying is panko. These Japanese-style crumbs have lots of texture, which I like to tone down a bit by crushing half of the crumbs with my hands before dredging.

There are several different methods you can use to apply bread crumbs. The standard French method is a three-step process, in which you first dip the food in flour, then in egg (sometimes egg and milk), before finally dredging in bread crumbs. Many Southern cooks call for a dip in buttermilk prior to a fine flour coating, or you can keep it even simpler by just rolling the food in flour or cornmeal. My favorite method is to dip the food to be fried in a mixture of two parts vinegar to one part water, shake dry, then roll in finely ground cornmeal.

The key to getting a crisp crust and a properly cooked interior is making sure that the bread coating is dry, which will prevent it from absorbing oil in the cooking process. To accomplish this, items should be breaded immediately before frying. All seafood that is fried should be skin off, as the skin can prevent the breading from adhering.

Properly fried foods are well flavored but not greasy to the touch. Use a narrow, deep pan, so there is enough oil for the foods to be fully submerged. When frying, you want to avoid overcrowding the pan or cooking at too low a temperature, as this is what causes foods to be greasy. A deep-fry thermometer, available at any kitchen supply shop or grocery store, is vital to this process, as oil gives little indication of its temperature the way water does. I think seafood is best deep-fried between 350°F and 375°F.

Knowing when fried foods are done requires a bit of practice, though it is not complicated. When frying seafood, generally you are cooking smaller pieces, and once the crust becomes golden brown and crisp and the vigorous bubbling has subsided, the seafood is usually done.

Note: All seafood categories described above are suitable to frying technique.

FRITTO MISTO WITH RED PEPPER COULIS

I prefer fried seafood as an appetizer, as it can be too much to eat an entire entrée's worth. This dish is the exception, as it incorporates so many unique and charismatic ingredients in addition to seafood, giving you so many textures that will keep your palate interested throughout eating the dish.

Lightly salt a selection of mixed seafood and vegetables—any seafood is appropriate, especially fresh sardine fillets, tinned anchovies, pickled herring, fresh squid, scallops, flounder, or mullet, sliced into finger-sized pieces—for roughly 10 to 15 minutes prior to use. Fry like ingredients together, dipping each piece separately in the batter.

Depending on the size of your pot, preheat 1 to 2 quarts peanut oil to 375°F. This dish is wonderful served at room temperature, so fry in small batches, as there is no need to rush. Line a large platter with newspaper or paper towels. Make a tempura batter by combining 1 cup of sifted flour, 2 tablespoons of sifted cornstarch, 1½ cups of seltzer water, and salt to taste. Whisk until smooth. Use within 10 minutes. If extra batter is required, simply whip up another batch.

One piece at a time, place in the hot oil, holding it for 5 seconds before releasing. Cook in small batches until golden and crispy. Turn with a slotted spoon if necessary to evenly cook both sides. Remove items as they finish and place on a lined platter to absorb excess oil. Repeat until all ingredients have been fried. It's best to save the stronger-flavored ingredients, such as sardines, until the end. Serve the Fritto Misto with Red Pepper Coulis (see page 244).

Using Peanut Oil

Because cooking oils react to heat differently, it's important to know which oil to reach for when you're sautéing, searing, or frying. When making a dish such as sautéed zucchini with garlic, which is cooked over moderate heat, I always use olive oil. The oil both absorbs the flavor of the garlic and mixes with the liquid released by the zucchini, which emulsifies into a rich and flavorful sauce. In such preparations, the flavor of the oil matters. Thus, olive oil is the perfect choice.

Searing ingredients at very high heat requires an oil that will not burn or develop a bitter flavor when exposed to extreme heat. In this case, the oil will not be part of the final dish, so there is no reason to use oil with a pronounced personality. Peanut and vegetables oils do the job well.

Frying requires an oil with similar qualities. Peanut oil is the very best for frying. Not only can it withstand high temperatures, but it also imparts a very slight, pleasant flavor to the crust. A major benefit of peanut oil is that it does not readily absorb the flavors of foods fried in it, which means that it can be used again without sharing a (possibly unpleasant!) remembrance of foods past. To re-use, strain the cooled oil through a fine mesh strainer to remove any particles. The oil can be used again for up to a week. I do not recommend using the same oil more than twice.

FRIED OYSTER PO' BOYS

Place 1 cup of flour in a bowl and season with a few tablespoons of Creole Seasoning (page 253) or Old Bay Seasoning. Whisk together 2 tablespoons of milk and 2 egg yolks in a second bowl. Place 1½ cups of fine cornmeal in a third bowl.

Fry until crisp and golden brown, 3 to 4 minutes. Transfer to the lined bowl and drain. Repeat until all the oysters have been fried.

Heat oil to 375°. Working in batches, dredge the oysters in the flour to fully coat. Transfer to the egg mixture and toss to fully coat. Transfer to the cornmeal and toss until fully coated. Drop the oysters, one at a time, into the hot oil.

For ideas on assembling and finishing Po' Boys, see page 89.

BOIL

Shellfish

Since fish is so delicate, it is not often boiled, but shellfish and crustaceans are perfectly suited to this method. Their shells help to protect the meat, keeping it moist while adding flavor. Boiling is also a great way to infuse the food with other flavors, such as Old Bay Seasoning, Creole Seasoning (see page 253), seaweed, and/or even seawater.

To boil crustaceans, first figure out how many people are coming over. This is important, as these types of gatherings tend to grow! The key to a good shellfish boil is a very large pot and a very powerful flame. I have a turkey fryer that I like to pull it out for these big boils. To start, add water and whatever flavorings you want to the pot and bring it to a boil. How much water? Enough to cover about half of the shellfish you intend to cook in it. All liquids should be heavily salted. Add your crustaceans and cover. Once the water returns to a boil, cook for the stated time (which is a general recommendation, as it all depends on the size of the pot, flame, and type of crustacean). If you like, cook the seafood in batches, as you'll have a little better control over its doneness.

SUGGESTED FLAVORINGS:

Pickling spices

Celery

Fennel

Onion

Carrot

Sausage

Lemons

Chile peppers

Seaweed

Creole Seasoning (page 253)

Old Bay Seasoning

Beer

Crabs

BLUE CRAB: The king of the Chesapeake is the crab I grew up on—small, feisty, ornery. Boiled with lager and Old Bay Seasoning, it's what a lot of my youth tasted like. Cook for 10 to 15 minutes.

DUNGENESS: Born of cold, deep waters, the quintessential West Coast crab boasts an incredibly intricate flavor. I must admit, it's somewhat more fun to eat than the blue crab, since your effort is rewarded by a generous yield. But picking crabs is never a lazy man's task. Dungeness are particularly good with lemon and pickling spices. Cook 1½- to 2½-pound crabs for 15 to 18 minutes; 3-pound crabs take about 20 minutes.

KING CRAB LEGS: These true delicacies may or may not be worth the potentially deadly trip out to catch them, but they are certainly worth a trip to the store where they are almost always marketed as frozen and precooked. These need only be warmed through—they are wonderful reheated in water that has been spiked with jalapeño and beer. Boil for 5 to 7 minutes.

JONAH/PEEKY TOE CRAB: This modestly flavored crab is not widely available outside of New England, but if you already came for the lobster, you might as well try a crab, too. These are particularly good cooked with seaweed in seawater and benefit from a little bit of spicy kick in the mix. Boil for 12 to 15 minutes.

Crawfish

The traditional way to cook crawfish, aka crawdads or mudbugs, in Louisiana is to bring the water and seasonings to a boil, drop in the crawfish, and simmer for 20 minutes, then remove from the heat and let sit for another 20-40 minutes to absorb the flavor. I like my crawfish fiery, and I season the water with lots of chile pepper and lemons.

Lobster

Maine lobster truly is a thing of beauty, but that doesn't mean it can't get down and dirty. I love cooking lobster with nontraditional ingredients like linguiça sausage, lots of limes, and spicy dried chiles. The key to any great boiled lobster is cooking it in seawater and fresh seaweed, but if that's not an option, adding dried seaweed and lots of sea salt to the water will suffice.

LOBSTER COOKING TIMES:

1 pound	7 minutes
1¼ pounds	9 minutes
1½ pounds	10 minutes
1¾ pounds	11 minutes
2 pounds	12 minutes
2½ pounds	14 minutes

Shrimp

Wild-caught U.S. shrimp are far and away the best-tasting shrimp to be had. My second choice is domestically farmed product. Shrimp work well with just about any seasoning, but their incredible sweetness takes especially to citrus, bold spices, and fiery heat. These spices encourage another great aspect of any boil: drinking copious quantities of ice-cold beer. Boil shell-on shrimp for suggested time per pound. Turn off the heat and allow to rest in the water for another 5 minutes.

Small (21–25 count)	2–4 minutes
Medium (16–20 count)	3–5 minutes
Large (10–15 count)	4–6 minutes

GRILL

I find that most people tend to enjoy seafood more in the summer months, which coincides with prime grilling season. Indeed, grilling is my favorite way to prepare seafood, but not all seafood works on the grill. No matter the cooking method, I believe that seafood rarely benefits from prolonged super high heat applications, so when it comes to grilling, I prefer to cook over indirect heat. I start the seafood on a grate that has been heated directly over high heat, but then quickly rotate the grate away from the high heat, allowing the fish to cook slowly while absorbing the rustic, smoky notes of live fire heat. I often place the cover on the grill, which captures the rising heat and creates an oven effect that evenly and gently cooks the fish from all sides. There is no need to turn the fish, so chances of the fish breaking or sticking are greatly reduced.

Seafood destined for the grill definitely benefits from a quick soak in a brine. For more on brining, see page 206.

Addition of Smoke

Most seafood tastes wonderful with a hint of smoke flavor, but the type of wood used matters greatly. Woods such as hickory and mesquite can totally overpower more delicately flavored seafood. Orchard, alder, and nut woods, such as pecan and almond, are all wonderful companions to the seafood grill. Just as I love peaches, my favorite wood for grilling is that of the peach tree. In my opinion, it's the queen of the bunch.

Grill Setup

Use a charcoal chimney with newspaper and ignite. Pour all
the coals to one side of the grill and add wood chips.

TROUT FILLETS WITH AILLADE

Best for Orange-Fleshed Fish, Mild to Medium and Full-Flavored Fillet Fish, Steak Fish

Note: *Steak fish is not often cooked with its skin. If using a steak fish, the steaks should be briefly seared on each side over the coals before being placed on the grate away from the fire to finish cooking.*

Do not move the fish, but rather rotate the grill grate with tongs so the fillets are opposite the coals. Cover the grill. The fish will cook one side up; do not flip. Once fillet is cooked, remove from grill.

Season fillet generously with salt. Place skin side down directly over coals and cook for 2 minutes.

After a few minutes (see Canadian Rule page 175), remove fillet from the grill. Serve trout fillet with Aillade (see page 241).

GRILLED WHOLE PERCH WITH BASIL OIL

Best for Mild to Medium and Full-Flavored Fillet Fish and Trout

Marinate the whole pan-dressed fish in Vinaigrette (see page 239). Place the whole fish on the grill, directly over coals, and cook 4 to 5 minutes. Rotate the grill grate so the fish is opposite the coals. Flip the fish gently using tongs and a spatula. Cover the grill and cook for 10 to 15 minutes until the fillet flakes under gentle pressure from your thumb.

Transfer the fish to a platter. Serve with Vibrant Basil Oil (see page 225).

GRILLED SARDINE SKEWERS
Best for Small Silver Fish

Place the skewers, skin side down, directly over the coals. Cook until the skin begins to char and crisp, about 2 minutes.

Stir together the finely grated zest of ½ lemon, 1 tablespoon of chopped mint, 1½ teaspoons of chopped tarragon, and 1 tablespoon of olive oil. Add the sardines, smelts, or any small silver fish and marinate.

Within 3 to 4 minutes the fish will be cooked through. Remove the skewers from the grill and serve.

BRINE WITH VARIATIONS

Given the delicate nature of seafood and its fragile muscular structures I have taken to brining almost all fish before cooking. Here's why: Brining more evenly seasons the fillet, as salt from the brine passes, through osmosis, into the cells of the fish. The salt strengthens the cell walls, and thus less moisture is lost. I also brine because it slightly stiffens the fragile flesh, giving a bit more structural integrity to fillets during cooking. This is especially important in cooking methods that require plenty of handling, such as stewing or grilling, which offer more opportunities for breaking the fillet. Brine times vary, due to the thickness or density of the fillet. A very dense fish like sturgeon or cobia will require a bit more time than thin, looser structured fillets like trout or sardines. I brine my seafood anywhere from 10 to 40 minutes. The brine itself can also be adjusted to be a little less potent, thus allowing its effects to be applied over a longer period of time. While the brines below work with any seafood, the stronger flavored brines better flatter fuller flavored fish. Once used, the brine should be discarded.

BASIC BRINE

2 cups water, divided use

1 tablespoon salt

1 tablespoon sugar

Heat 1 cup of the water in a small saucepan until steaming. Add the salt and sugar, stirring to dissolve. Add the remaining water and chill before using.

To brine seafood, ensure that the fillets are completely submerged in the brine. Once the brine time has been reached, remove the fillets and pat dry. Reserve until ready to use. Discard the brine.

PERNOD VARIATION

Add 1 tablespoon of Pernod (or other anise-flavored liquor) to the recipe and proceed as above.

HERB OR SPICE VARIATION

Adding herbs or spices such as fennel seed or juniper to a brine is a great way to subtly introduce their flavors to a dish. To do so, bring 1 cup of the water to a steaming point, then plunge the herbs and/or spices into it. Allow them to steep for 5 minutes or so before combining with the remaining 1 cup of water, salt, and sugar. Cool the brine completely before using on fish.

UMAMI-KELP VARIATION

Many seagreens have high levels of compounds rich in umami, the fifth taste, and the addition of just a small amount of seagreens in a brine solution can further accentuate the seafood's natural flavors.

To infuse kelp in a brine, heat 1 cup of the water until steaming. Add about 1 tablespoon of crumbled dried kelp, the salt, and the sugar. Stir to dissolve, then add the remaining 1 cup of water. Cool completely before using. Strain out the kelp before adding fish to the brine.

SMOKE

The art of smoking seafood is just that—an art. There are so many variables that come into play: the type of fish and its fattiness, cure type, drying time, and whether you want a hot or cold smoked product. As a warning though, some seafood can turn quite tinny in taste when smoked flavor is applied. I recommend sticking to the wide variety of seafood already available in smoked form as a guideline for what you should smoke at home: salmon, mackerel, trout, bluefish, sturgeon, herring, and so on.

Smoked fish requires a stronger brine than those listed above. For hot smoking, I tend to use a very strong brine and a lengthy drying process of up to 1 day. As always, a little sprinkling of Pernod is a friendly companion, especially when applied just before meeting the smoke.

HOT-SMOKED MACKEREL

Best for Full-Flavored Fillet Fish, Small Silver Fish, Orange-Fleshed Fish

Hot smoked seafood is fully cooked over moderate heat. Use a small amount of charcoal and wood chips or chunks.

Prepare a brine of 2 cups of water, 2 tablespoons of red wine vinegar, 2 tablespoons of brown sugar, 1½ tablespoons of salt, and 1 teaspoon of garlic powder (see Brine with Variations, page 206, for the method). When the brine has cooled completely, add 2 pounds of butterflied mackerel (backbone removed) or large fillets. Brine for 30 minutes.

Remove the fish from the brine and arrange flesh-side up on a rack. Refrigerate, uncovered, for at least 1 hour and up to overnight to dry.

Prepare a hot smoker to roughly 200°F, preferably with alder or applewood. Either lay the fillets on a rack or skewer and hang.

Smoke until the fillets are deeply amber hued and cooked through, about 45 minutes to an hour, adding more woods chips as needed. Remove from the smoker. Let cool completely before serving or storing. The smoked fish will last up to 3 days in the refrigerator, covered.

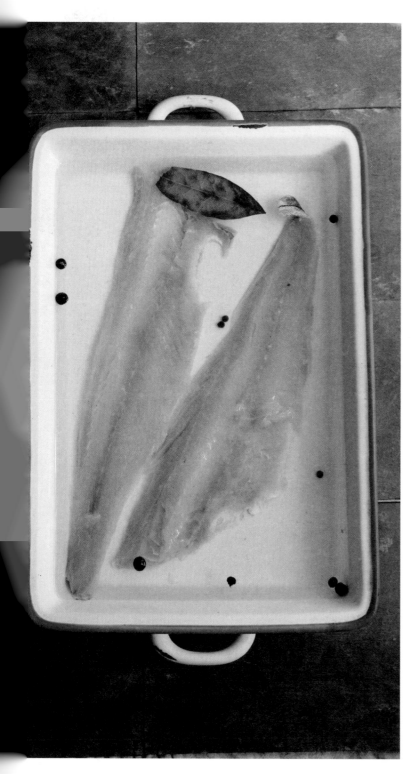

FINNAN HADDIE
(COLD SMOKE METHOD)

Best for Flaky White-Fleshed Fish, Orange-Fleshed Fish

SERVES 4

Cold smoking is when seafood is flavored with smoke but is not cooked. When eating cold smoked seafood you should take the same precautions as when eating raw seafood. (See page 32.) While recipes to make your own Finnan Haddie can require a day or more to complete, this recipe can be made in just a couple hours. The longer method will produce richer and more elegant flavors as the smoke softens its personality with a bit more time, but the quick prep is so easy and very charming.

To prepare for cold smoking, over a small amount of charcoal ignite a small amount of sawdust or wood chips, as these will produce less heat. Fill an oven-safe dish with ice and place directly over the fire to help cool the rising smoke.

Bring 1 cup of water to a boil in a small saucepan. Add ⅓ cup of kosher salt, ¼ cup of sugar, 5 peppercorns, 5 allspice or juniper berries, and 1 bay leaf, stirring to dissolve the salt and sugar. Remove from the heat and add 3 cups water to the brine. Refrigerate the brine until cold.

Lay 1½ pounds of haddock fillets (skin on, pin bones removed) in a roasting dish in a single layer. Pour the chilled brine over the fish; the fillets should be completely submerged in the brine (add a bit more water if necessary, or use a smaller pan). Refrigerate for 1½ hours.

Prepare a smoker or grill for the cold smoke process. Add a handful of sawdust or chips to the fire and proceed to smoke the fish for about 45 minutes, which may require one to three additions of wood, depending on the burn rate.

Remove the fillets (discard the brine), pat dry, and lay on a wire rack (preferably that of your smoker). Let dry, uncovered, in the refrigerator for at least 1 hour but as long as overnight. This will allow the flesh to dry out a little and a tacky film to develop that will help the smoke flavor penetrate.

Remove the now ruddy-toned fish and refrigerate, uncovered, for at least 1 hour and up to 1 day for the flavors to meld. The fish can be used at this point or wrapped tightly in multiple layers of plastic wrap and frozen until needed.

SAUCES

Pristine seafood doesn't require a sauce—on its own, it is as gorgeous a food as we are lucky to have, offering an impressive variety of taste, texture, and nuance. But some fish benefit from hearty flavors to accentuate their personality. Others need only a subtle accompaniment to really shine. Of the sauces that follow, some represent tradition while others are more modern in their character. Most pair well with other foods, be it vegetables, chicken, or meat, and can be made ahead. So take a look through and pick a couple you like. While certainly not comprehensive, this collection of recipes is a good guide to the compelling range of flavors that you can easily incorporate into your routine.

Butter versus Olive Oil

Just as you ponder whether your meal might be better paired with Cabernet or Chardonnay, so too should you think whether a particular seafood pairs better with olive oil or butter. Because seafood generally is a very lean protein, the inclusion of a fat, usually as a finishing drizzle or in a sauce, is traditional. That said, these two fats have very different personalities, and one is often a better match for a given seafood. Butter mellows and binds seafood's flavor to other ingredients, giving the dish a mellow and delicate profile in which the seafood can shine. Olive oil, with its grassy, herbal, or fruity notes, offers greater contrast, drawing out more pronounced flavors, such as the briny punctuation of scallops or clams. It's worth experimenting to see what you like better with any given species.

LOUISIANA RÉMOULADE

MAKES ABOUT 1½ CUPS

Bright and spunky, this rémoulade is very different from the ubiquitous mayo-based version. Serve it with poached, slow-roasted, grilled, or broiled shellfish and fish.

½ cup vegetable oil

2 tablespoons red wine vinegar

1 tablespoon prepared horseradish

1 tablespoon chopped tarragon

1 tablespoon finely chopped flat-leaf parsley

1 tablespoon smoked sweet paprika

1 scallion, finely chopped

1 clove garlic, minced

1 anchovy fillet, chopped

1 teaspoon whole grain mustard

Whisk all ingredients together until thoroughly combined. Let rest at least 1 hour or refrigerate up to 3 days (longer than that and the garlic gets too punchy). It will separate as it sits, so give a quick stir before serving.

NOLA RÉMOULADE

MAKES ABOUT 1½ CUPS

This creamier version goes well with grilled or broiled full-flavored seafoods.

Juice of ½ lemon

2 teaspoons prepared
horseradish

2 teaspoons mustard
powder

1½ teaspoons smoked
sweet paprika

½ teaspoon celery seeds

A pinch ground cloves

2 tablespoons water

½ cup vegetable oil

2 celery stalks, finely diced

½ teaspoon whole grain
mustard

Combine the lemon juice, horseradish, mustard powder, paprika, celery seeds, cloves, and water in a blender. With the motor running, slowly drizzle in the oil and blend until thickened and emulsified. Remove from blender, and stir in the celery and whole grain mustard. The rémoulade keeps up to 2 days in the refrigerator.

(NOT SO) CLASSIC RÉMOULADE

MAKES ABOUT 2 CUPS

Swapping Greek yogurt for mayonnaise makes this rémoulade healthier, yes, but also a great deal zippier. Serve it with fried, pan-fried, or boiled shellfish.

1 (7-ounce) container plain Greek yogurt

1 teaspoon Creole or whole grain mustard

1 teaspoon Worcestershire sauce

1 clove garlic, minced

2 tablespoons chopped scallions

2 tablespoons finely chopped shallot

2 tablespoons finely diced celery

2 tablespoons chopped flat-leaf parsley

Salt and pepper to taste

Whisk together the yogurt, mustard, Worcestershire sauce, and garlic until thoroughly combined and smooth. Stir in the scallions, shallot, celery, and parsley. Season with salt and pepper. Let sit for 1 hour before serving. The remoulade keeps up to 2 days in the refrigerator.

TARTAR SAUCE

MAKES ABOUT 1½ CUPS

Of course, this classic sauce pairs well with any type of fried or pan-fried seafood, but it's also delicious smeared in a Po' Boy or used as a salad dressing for hearty, crunchy veggies.

1 egg yolk

¼ cup finely grated Parmesan

1 tablespoon red wine vinegar

1 teaspoon capers, rinsed and drained

2 teaspoons Dijon mustard

½ cup olive oil

½ cup vegetable oil

8 gherkins, finely diced

Combine the egg yolk, Parmesan, vinegar, capers, and mustard in a blender or food processor. Purée for a few seconds, then slowly drizzle in the olive oil and vegetable oil until thick and emulsified. Remove from the blender and stir in the gherkins. The tartar sauce keeps for up to 4 days in the refrigerator.

COCKTAIL SAUCE

MAKES ABOUT ¾ CUP

This kicky sauce is delicious with poached shellfish or fried seafood of any kind.

½ cup chili sauce

1 tablespoon prepared horseradish

2 teaspoons Worcestershire sauce

2 teaspoons vinegar-based hot sauce, such as Tapatio® brand

Pinch of salt

Stir all ingredients to combine. The cocktail sauce keeps for up to 5 days in the refrigerator.

INFUSED VINEGARS

These infusions are a great pick-me-up to almost any dish, with the bright vinegar and aromatic herbs adding interest and complexity. Use as you would a common hot sauce, drizzling a few teaspoons over a finished dish.

These herb infusions should be made fresh in small batches, and then kept in the fridge for up to 1 week. Keep the herbs whole (so they can be removed easily) and, using the back of a knife, lightly bruise the leaves and stalk. Combine the herbs with the vinegar and let steep for a couple of hours for the flavors to meld. Heartier herbs such as rosemary should steep a little less.

Some suggested combinations:

White wine vinegar with chervil

Red wine vinegar with thyme or tarragon

White balsamic vinegar with dill

Balsamic vinegar with rosemary

Sherry vinegar with mint

CHILE OIL

Drizzle this rusty-hued oil over a finished fish dish for a little extra verve and gentle heat.

¼ cup pure olive oil
or mild extra-virgin
olive oil

1 teaspoon smoked
sweet paprika

Small pinch of
Aleppo, Espelette,
or other flavorful
dried chile flakes

Combine the ingredients in a small saucepan and heat very gently over the lowest setting possible. Let warm for about 10 minutes and remove from the heat. Transfer to a jar or bowl and cool completely. Let sit for a couple of days before using, allowing the oil to extract the perfume and personality of the paprika and spice. Before using, allow the paprika to settle to the bottom and use only the clear oil on top. The chile oil keeps for up to 3 weeks.

ORANGE-SPICED OLIVE OIL

MAKES ½ CUP

This infused olive oil is great with rich, grilled fish, especially in the cooler autumn months.

4 tablespoons extra-virgin olive oil

Zest of 1 orange

4 whole cloves

A pinch ground cinnamon

A pinch crushed red chile flakes, such as nora or dried chipotle

4 tablespoons chopped flat-leaf parsley

Gently warm the oil in a small saucepan over low heat. Add the orange zest, cloves, cinnamon, and chile flakes and let steep for at least 2 hours and up to 1 day. Strain, then stir the parsley into the oil. Refrigerated, the oil keeps for up to 2 days.

VIBRANT BASIL OIL

MAKES ABOUT ½ CUP

Fresh basil, finely chopped to release its precious character, is steeped in sweet olive oil and refrigerated until solid. The resulting sauce has the texture of spreadable butter. Invite guests to spoon out a generous portion of the murky and mysterious oil and dollop on their fish. As it melts, the oil will run across the fillet, leaving in its wake a beautiful mosaic of deep green flecks. The basil will bloom again from the heat of the fish, its vibrancy a welcome remembrance of summer some chilly evening.

3 sprigs fresh basil, preferably Genovese, leaves only

⅓ cup extra-virgin olive oil, preferably a buttery Spanish varietal such as arbequina or picual

Finely grated zest of ½ lemon

Pinch of salt

Stack half of the basil leaves and then roll them into a cigar-like tube. Using a very sharp knife, cut the rolled leaves crosswise into very thin strips. As you cut, keep the strips neatly in order. Gently turn these strips 90° and cut the rolled leaves lengthwise. (By doing so you will produce a very finely minced basil, but it will not be bruised or tired, its flavors surrendered to the cutting board.)

Gently warm the olive oil in a small saucepan over moderate heat for just a minute. Remove from the heat and add the lemon zest, salt, and chopped basil. Stir to combine, then transfer to a small jar or ramekin for serving. Place the jar in the refrigerator for at least 3 hours and up to 1 week. Just prior to serving, allow the oil to thaw slightly, but do not let it melt.

HERBES DE PROVENCE OIL

MAKES ABOUT ⅓ CUP

Use this as a finishing oil, drizzling a little over a dish just before serving. Its herbaceous aroma goes well with practically any seafood.

⅓ cup extra-virgin olive oil

1 teaspoon fennel seeds

2 sprigs fresh mint, leaves only

1 sprig fresh oregano

1 sprig fresh marjoram

1 sprig fresh thyme

½ sprig fresh rosemary

A few leaves fresh lavender

Combine the olive oil and fennel seed in a small saucepan over low heat and heat gently until the rich fennel aroma begins to bloom, about 5 minutes. Remove from the heat and let cool for a few minutes.

Using the back side of a knife, bruise the mint, oregano, marjoram, thyme, rosemary, and lavender by gently pounding them on a cutting board. This must be a very gentle action—you want to "wake up" the herbs without muddying their flavor.

Gently pack the herbs into a small jar. Pour in the olive oil and fennel seeds. Cover the jar and shake vigorously for 20 seconds. Let the oil sit at room temperature for 15 to 30 minutes, then strain. The oil will keep for up to 2 days.

FURIKAKE
(SEAWEED SEASONING)

MAKES ABOUT ½ CUP

Used as a finishing salt for any dish, this recipe makes a generous quantity that can be used for up to 2 weeks.

¼ cup sesame seeds

3 sheets nori

2 tablespoons bonito flakes

Pinch of crushed red chile flakes

1 teaspoon ground coriander

1 teaspoon onion powder

Toast the sesame seeds in a sauté pan over medium-low heat, shaking the pan and watching them carefully, until warmed through and fragrant, 4 to 5 minutes. Transfer the seeds to a small bowl and reserve.

Tear the nori sheets into 6 to 8 pieces. Working in batches, add the nori to the pan and toast over medium heat until the seaweed becomes brighter green, about 2 minutes. Transfer the nori to a plate.

Add the bonito flakes ,to the pan and toast until fragrant, about 30 seconds. Transfer to a small bowl.

Using a mortar and pestle, crush half of the sesame seeds. When these are a chunky paste, add the chile flakes, coriander, onion powder, toasted nori, and bonito flakes, and grind until the mixture is well combined and the ingredients are all about the same size. Stir in the reserved sesame seeds. Store the mixture in a sealed plastic bag until ready to use (up to 2 weeks).

SALMORIGLIO

MAKES ABOUT 1 CUP

This southern Italian specialty pulls double duty. It works equally well as a marinade for grilled or griddled fish and as a sauce for grilled, broiled, poached, and baked seafood.

2 shallots, peeled and
roughly chopped

2 cloves garlic

½ bunch flat-leaf parsley,
leaves only, chopped

2 sprigs fresh tarragon,
leaves only

2 sprigs fresh oregano,
leaves only

Salt to taste

¼ cup olive oil

Combine all the ingredients in a food processor and pulse to form a paste. Alternatively, use a mortar pestle to crush by hand. The sauce keeps up to 2 days.

AVOCADO AND POMEGRANATE SALSA

MAKES ABOUT 2 CUPS

Cubes of creamy avocado and tart, popping pomegranate seeds come together in this beautiful salsa that works for any grilled, broiled, or sautéed fish, though it's especially great with salmon.

1 avocado, pitted, peeled, and diced into ⅓-inch cubes

Seeds of ½ pomegranate

Juice of ½ lemon

2 tablespoons extra-virgin olive oil

Salt

Freshly ground pepper-allspice

Gently stir together the avocado, pomegranate seeds, lemon juice, and olive oil. Season to taste with salt and pepper–allspice. Serve immediately.

COMPOUND BUTTERS

These flavored butters are shaped into logs and frozen. To serve, pull from the freezer, cut off slices, and place them directly on a piece of hot fish. The butter will melt, coating bright flavor all over the fish.

BEURRE BLANC STYLE

MAKES ENOUGH FOR 4 SERVINGS

½ cup white wine

1½ teaspoons finely chopped shallot

1 sprig fresh thyme

3 peppercorns

1 allspice berry

4 tablespoons butter, cut into small cubes

4 teaspoons finely chopped flat-leaf parsley

1 teaspoon finely grated lemon zest

Pinch of cayenne

Combine the wine, shallots, thyme, peppercorns, and allspice in a small pan and simmer over medium heat until the wine has reduced to about 3 tablespoons. Remove from the heat and strain into a bowl, pressing on the solids to extract every drop of liquid. Discard the solids.

Add the butter, parsley, lemon zest, and cayenne to the warm wine, and swirl to incorporate the ingredients and melt the butter. Cool completely until solid.

Shape the butter into a log, wrap tightly in plastic wrap, and freeze until ready to use.

ROUGE STYLE

MAKES ENOUGH FOR 4 SERVINGS

½ cup red wine

1½ teaspoons finely chopped shallot

1 sprig fresh thyme

3 peppercorns

1 allspice berry

4 tablespoons butter, cut into small cubes

4 teaspoons fresh chervil

1 teaspoon finely grated orange zest

Pinch of cayenne

Combine the wine, shallots, thyme, peppercorns, and allspice in a small pan and simmer over medium heat until the wine has reduced to about 3 tablespoons. Remove from the heat and strain into a bowl, pressing on the solids to extract every drop of liquid. Discard the solids.

Add the butter, chervil, orange zest, and cayenne to the warm wine and swirl to incorporate the ingredients and melt the butter. Cool completely until solid.

Shape the butter into a log, wrap tightly in plastic wrap, and freeze until ready to use.

SORREL BUTTER

MAKES ENOUGH FOR 4 SERVINGS

4 tablespoons butter, softened

3 tablespoons finely chopped fresh sorrel

1 tablespoon heavy cream

Salt

Combine the butter, sorrel, and cream in a bowl and season with salt. Whisk vigorously until thoroughly combined.

Shape the butter into a log, wrap tightly in plastic wrap, and freeze until ready to use.

GARLIC BUTTER

MAKES ENOUGH FOR 4 SERVINGS

6 garlic cloves, peeled

4 tablespoons butter, softened

1 teaspoon red wine vinegar

Pinch of cayenne

Salt

Bring a small pot of water to a boil, add the garlic, and boil for 5 minutes. Drain and cool completely.

Combine the butter, vinegar, cayenne, and reserved garlic in a bowl and season with salt. Whisk vigorously until thoroughly combined.

Shape the butter into a log, wrap tightly in plastic wrap, and freeze until ready to use.

SEAWEED BUTTER

MAKES ENOUGH FOR 4 SERVINGS

4 tablespoons butter, softened

1 tablespoon flaked dried kelp or dulse

1 teaspoon Pernod or other anise-flavored liquor

Salt

Freshly ground pepper-allspice

Combine the butter, kelp, and Pernod in a bowl and season with salt and pepper–allspice. Whisk vigorously until thoroughly combined.

Shape the butter into a log, wrap tightly in plastic wrap, and freeze until ready to use.

ANCHOVY BUTTER

MAKES ENOUGH FOR 4 SERVINGS

2 anchovy fillets, minced

4 tablespoons butter, softened

1 tablespoon mayonnaise

1 tablespoon chopped fresh tarragon or chervil

Pinch of cayenne

Lemon juice to taste

Combine the anchovies, butter, mayonnaise, tarragon, and cayenne in a bowl and season with a few drops of lemon juice. Whisk vigorously until thoroughly combined.

Shape the butter into a log, wrap tightly in plastic wrap, and freeze until ready to use.

SHRIMP BUTTER

MAKES ENOUGH FOR 8 SERVINGS

8 tablespoons (1 stick) butter, softened, divided use

1 sprig fresh thyme, leaves only, chopped

1 clove garlic, grated

1 teaspoon tomato paste

1 teaspoon fennel seeds, crushed using the bottom of a heavy pot

½ teaspoon onion powder

6 shrimp, finely minced

Heat 2 tablespoons of the butter in a sauté pan over medium heat. Add the thyme, garlic, tomato paste, fennel seeds, and onion powder and stir to combine. Cook for 4 minuites. Add the shrimp and cook, stirring occasionally, until cooked through, about 4 minutes. Remove from the heat and transfer the mixture to a bowl. Add the remaining butter and whisk vigorously until thoroughly combined.

Shape the butter into a log, wrap tightly in plastic wrap, and freeze until ready to use.

VINAIGRETTE

MAKES ½ CUP

Salad? Obviously. But a classic vinaigrette also makes a perfect sauce for any seafood preparation.

1 tablespoon red or white wine vinegar or balsamic vinegar

1 teaspoon mustard powder

1 clove garlic, grated

1 sprig fresh thyme, leaves only

Salt

3 tablespoons extra-virgin olive oil (2 tablespoons if using balsamic vinegar)

Combine the vinegar, mustard powder, garlic, thyme, and a pinch of salt in a bowl. Add the olive oil and whisk to incorporate. Let sit for 10 minutes before using.

MARINATED ORANGE SEGMENTS WITH CHILE

MAKES ABOUT 1 CUP

Grilled and broiled fish are wonderful topped with this refreshing sweet-sour mix of citrus, rich olive oil, and serrano chile.

2 oranges, peeled and segmented

1 serrano chile, very thinly sliced

1 shallot, very thinly sliced

Salt

2 tablespoons extra-virgin olive oil

2 teaspoons sherry vinegar

Combine the orange segments, chile, shallot, and salt to taste in a colander. Let sit and drain for 15 minutes. Transfer the mixture to a bowl and combine with the vinegar and olive oil. Gently stir to incorporate. Use immediately.

SKORDALIA

MAKES ABOUT 2 CUPS

The woodsy, toasty personality of this sauce makes it a great foil for rich seafoods such as seared scallops or butter-basted fillets.

¾ cup slivered almonds

3 cloves garlic, halved

1 sprig fresh rosemary, leaves only, stem discarded

1 tablespoon extra-virgin olive oil

1 egg yolk

1 tablespoon sherry vinegar

1 cup pure olive oil or vegetable oil

Salt

Preheat the oven to 375°F. Spread the almonds and garlic on a small baking sheet and roast for 5 minutes. Add the rosemary to the baking sheet and drizzle the extra-virgin olive oil over everything. Roast 5 minutes more. Remove from the oven and transfer the nut mixture to a food processor (or mortar and pestle). Pulse until ground. Transfer to a bowl and let cool completely. Add the egg yolk and vinegar to the nut mixture, then slowly whisk in the oil and season with salt. The *skordalia* keeps for 2 days.

AILLADE

MAKES ABOUT 1½ CUPS

I found inspiration for this sauce in an old Elizabeth David book. It cleverly uses the gentle heat of the toasted pistachios to soften the bite of garlic and help the lemon zest bloom, resulting in a textured, harmonious sauce that works with everything from grilled fish and roasted vegetables to risotto and pasta.

½ cup shelled pistachios

1 clove garlic, grated

Finely grated zest of 1 lemon

1 bunch parsley, leaves chopped (about 1 cup)

½ cup extra-virgin olive oil

Pinch crushed red chile flakes

Salt

Preheat the oven to 375°F. Arrange the pistachios on a small baking sheet and toast in the oven until aromatic, about 10 minutes. Remove from the oven and transfer to a food processor (or mortar and pestle). Add the garlic and lemon zest to the warm pistachios and pulse until ground. Transfer to a bowl and stir in the parsley, olive oil, and chile flakes. Season with salt to taste. The *aillade* can be made up to 1 day in advance and kept at room temperature.

RED PEPPER COULIS

MAKES ABOUT 2 CUPS

The sultry flavor and texture of roasted red pepper adds elegance to any dish it accompanies. I like to spike mine with vinegar and mint to ensure a super bright flavor. It's particularly good served with fried foods, as it helps to cut the richness.

2 red bell peppers, roasted, skinned, and seeded

2 tablespoons extra-virgin olive oil

2 tablespoons butter

1 tablespoon red wine vinegar

1 tablespoon chopped fresh mint

Salt to taste

Combine all ingredients in a blender and blend until smooth. The coulis can be made up to 1 day in advance. Serve at room temperature.

GREMOLATA

MAKES ABOUT ½ CUP

This simple combination of finely chopped parsley, lemon zest, and garlic is traditionally served over osso buco to cut its richness, but gremolata also adds a fresh grace note to grilled or roasted fish.

½ bunch flat-leaf parsley, leaves only

Finely grated zest of 1 lemon

1 small clove garlic, grated

Dash of ground mace

Salt

2 tablespoons extra-virgin olive oil, plus more for garnish

Finely chop the parsley leaves, then add the lemon zest and garlic and continue chopping until minced and well combined. Transfer the parsley mixture to a small bowl. Add the mace and salt to taste. Gently stir in the olive oil to make a fluffy paste, adding more oil if you want a saucier consistency. Use within a few hours.

CHERMOULA

MAKES ABOUT 2 CUPS

Despite the heavy hitters in the ingredient list, the final sauce is smooth and mellow. I particularly like it with full-flavored seafood, such as bluefish, tuna, or mackerel, and as a dipping sauce for whole seared sardines.

2 teaspoons smoked sweet paprika

1 teaspoon ground cumin

1 teaspoon ground coriander

1 serrano or jalapeño pepper, halved and seeds discarded

¼ cup parsley leaves

¼ cup mint leaves

¼ cup cilantro leaves

1 tablespoon finely grated fresh ginger

½ cup extra-virgin olive oil

Juice of ½ lemon

Salt to taste

Combine the paprika, cumin, and coriander in a small dry sauté pan over medium heat and toast, stirring, until very fragrant, about 2 minutes. Transfer to a food processor along with the remaining ingredients. Pulse until a paste forms. The *chermoula* can be made up to a day in advance.

SPICY MARINARA SAUCE

MAKES ABOUT 2 CUPS

I prefer a chunky marinara, but if you like a smoother sauce I suggest using a potato masher, twisting as you push down to produce a fine texture without defeating the character of the tomatoes. Do not use a blender or food processor—they are too powerful for the personality of this sauce and will change its color as they whip air into it.

6 tablespoons extra-virgin olive oil, divided use

4 dried Calabrian or árbol chiles

1 clove garlic, sliced

1 (14-ounce) can diced fire-roasted tomatoes

1 pod star anise or 1 stick cinnamon (optional)

Salt

Lemon juice to taste

Heat 4 tablespoons of the olive oil in a saucepan over medium-high heat. Add the chiles and garlic and cook until browned, about 5 minutes. Add the tomatoes and star anise or cinnamon, if using. Bring to a simmer and cook for 10 minutes. Remove from the heat.

Discard the star anise or cinnamon, if included, and, depending on your comfort level with spice, either fish out and discard the chiles or leave them in. Add the remaining 2 tablespoons of olive oil, and mash the tomatoes with back of a wooden spoon until lightly crushed. Season with salt and drops of lemon juice, if needed. The marinara can be kept for up to 2 days.

FRESH TOMATO SALSA

MAKES ABOUT 2 CUPS

A must for fish tacos, this straightforward salsa is also great over any grilled fish.

1 pint Sungold tomatoes, quartered

1½ tablespoons finely chopped red onion, briefly rinsed under cold water

¼ to 1 fresh chile pepper, such as jalapeño or serrano, seeds removed and finely chopped

¼ cup chopped cilantro

Juice of ½ lime

Salt to taste

Combine all ingredients in a bowl and gently mix together. Let sit for 1 hour or before serving.

HOMEMADE WORCESTERSHIRE SAUCE

MAKES ABOUT ½ CUP

Just like bitters invigorate cocktails, Worcestershire sauce adds a distinct depth and layered structure to sauces and braises. I use it all the time. My only complaint is that I find the store-bought stuff to be overly sweet, which can throw my dishes out of balance. So I came up with this version that's lighter on the sweetness and heavier on the anchovies. Go figure!

1 (2-ounce) can oil-packed anchovies, drained and minced

¼ cup apple cider vinegar

¼ cup water

1 tablespoon fish sauce

1 tablespoon soy sauce

1½ teaspoons molasses

2 cloves garlic, smashed

1 quarter-size knob fresh ginger

1 tablespoon dried seaweed flakes, such as dulse

4 juniper berries

2 whole cloves

1 teaspoon onion powder

Pinch of ground cinnamon

Pinch of cayenne or other well-flavored hot chile such as Aleppo or Espelette

Combine all the ingredients in a small saucepan and bring to a simmer over low heat. Gently simmer for 20 minutes. Remove from the heat and let sit for 20 minutes. Pour the sauce through a fine-mesh strainer and chill.

The sauce can be used at this point, but I think it's better to let it sit at least 1 day before using. It will keep, refrigerated, for up to 1 week.

BLACK BUTTER SAUCE

MAKES ENOUGH FOR 4 SERVINGS

Cooking butter until browned adds a dimension of nutty depth to everything it touches. This sauce is best paired with any flaky white fish.

6 tablespoons butter, divided use

1 sprig fresh thyme

Pinch of cayenne

1 tablespoon red or white wine vinegar

Salt

Heat 3 tablespoons of the butter in a small saucepan over medium heat until the butter has browned and black flecks have formed, 5 to 6 minutes. Add the thyme and cayenne and cook for just a few seconds. Remove from the heat and add the vinegar to stop the cooking. Swirl in the remaining 3 tablespoons of butter, adding a drop or two of water if needed to bring the sauce together. Use immediately.

CHILE VINEGAR HOT SAUCE

MAKES ABOUT 1 CUP

You can make large batches of this Southern-style hot sauce and heat-process it in sterilized jars. The sauce will continue to improve in flavor as it ages, but make sure to use it within 4 months. I like to douse fried or grilled fish with this stuff.

6 small dried chile peppers, such as árbol or Calabrian

1 cup distilled white vinegar

Salt

Toast the chiles in a dry pan over medium heat for 2 to 3 minutes. Add the vinegar and salt to taste, and cook until warm. Remove from the heat and transfer to a jar to cool. Let sit for at least 1 day and up to 1 month for flavors to develop.

WATERCRESS SAUCE

MAKES ABOUT 2 CUPS

This buttery sauce has a verdant bite to it. It's best served with pan-fried, sautéed, or broiled seafood.

8 tablespoons (1 stick)
butter, divided use

1 shallot, chopped

1 bunch watercress,
trimmed

2 tablespoons white wine
or water

Salt

Freshly ground
pepper-allspice

Heat 3 tablespoons of the butter in a small pan over medium heat. Add the shallots and cook until softened, about 3 minutes. Add the watercress, wine, and salt to taste and cook until wilted, about 2 minutes. Remove from the heat and transfer the mixture to a food processor or blender. Season with freshly ground pepper-allspice. Add the remaining 5 tablespoons of butter and purée until smooth. Serve the watercress sauce warm or chilled. It can be made up to a day in advance.

CREOLE SEASONING

MAKES ABOUT ¾ CUP

This is really a pretty straightforward recipe. Buy good spices, use them often, and throw them away if they've been sitting around for too long (as in those jars you inherited from your grandmother's kitchen). The potent flavors in this blend work best with full-flavored fishes such as mackerel and bluefish, but it's equally good with burgers or grilled chicken. It will keep in an airtight container for several weeks before losing some of its kick.

2 tablespoons salt

1½ tablespoons
smoked sweet paprika

1 tablespoon
dried oregano

1 tablespoon
onion powder

1 tablespoon
garlic powder

2 teaspoons ground
mustard powder

1 teaspoon crushed dried
chile pepper, such as
Nora or árbol

1 teaspoon ground mace

1 teaspoon
ground allspice

Combine all ingredients in a small bowl and stir well. This mix can be kept for up to 3 to 4 weeks sealed and stored in a cool, dark place.

CLASSIC AIOLI

MAKES ABOUT 2½ CUPS

Aioli is my mother sauce, one that I add to so many dishes in place of jarred mayonnaise. I make and keep large batches of it in the fridge. I like to flavor the aioli depending on its final use. For instance, I make a carrot dish in which I boil and then grill carrots until they reach a deeply charred sweetness. Aioli spiked with chopped tarragon makes an especially good accompaniment to this dish. No matter how you season your aioli, it's important to use very fresh garlic, as any bruised or aging cloves can lend an unpleasantly pronounced spicy zing.

Most herbs blend very well into any dish that aioli adorns. I like to use any combination of herbs, especially mint, tarragon, or tons of chopped fennel fronds. One of my favorite combinations is a salad of freshly shucked lima beans, boiled in salted water, and served with aioli spiked with the herb savory.

1 egg yolk

1 large clove garlic, grated

1½ teaspoons sherry vinegar

2 teaspoons salt

2 cups vegetable oil

1 tablespoon water

Combine the egg yolk, garlic, vinegar, and salt in a large bowl and whisk to combine. Place the bowl on a damp towel or have someone hold it for you to keep it steady. While whisking, slowly drizzle in the oil until the sauce emulsifies and thickens. As it thickens, add the water a few drops at a time (this will thin the aioli so that it can take more oil). Continue drizzling and whisking until all the oil has been incorporated. Yes, your arm may be a little tired, but this is definitely worth the effort. Aioli keeps in the refrigerator for up to 3 days.

If adding herbs to the aioli, simply stir in the chopped herbs after all of the oil has been added. Use herbed aioli within a day, though the herbs can be added to a classic aioli at any time.

FAKE AIOLI

MAKES ABOUT 1 CUP

If you don't have time to make aioli from scratch you can fake it by mixing mayonnaise and Greek yogurt with a dash of white vinegar and grated garlic. The garlic gives it just a hint of flair, and the Greek yogurt lends extra acid and verve.

½ cup mayonnaise

½ cup Greek yogurt

2 garlic cloves, grated

Dash of distilled white vinegar or white wine vinegar

Salt to taste

Combine all ingredients and whisk together until smooth. The sauce keeps in the refrigerator for up to 3 days.

ANCHOVY MAYONNAISE

MAKES ABOUT 1 CUP

Try dipping French fries into this savory, garlicky mayo—you'll never go back to ketchup.

1 (2-ounce) can oil-packed anchovies

½ cup Classic Aioli (page 257) or mayonnaise

1 tablespoon Worcestershire sauce

2 cloves garlic, grated

3 tablespoons chopped parsley

Put the anchovies with their oil in a bowl and mash until smooth. Whisk in the aioli and Worcestershire sauce, then fold in the garlic and parsley. The mayonnaise keeps, refrigerated, for up to 2 days.

BUTTERY SEAFOOD ESSENCE

MAKES ENOUGH FOR 4 SERVINGS

This is traditionally made from the liquid used to shallow poach fish (page 186). By using premade stock instead you can serve this with grilled, broiled, deep-poached, and slow-roasted seafoods.

1 cup Basic Fish Stock (page 93) or vegetable stock

½ cup white wine

5 tablespoons butter, cut into pieces

1 plum tomato, seeded and finely diced

2 tablespoons chopped herbs, such as tarragon, parsley, or chervil

Salt

Combine the stock and wine in a small saucepan and bring to a simmer over medium heat. Simmer until reduced to about 4 tablespoons. Remove from the heat and add the butter, tomato, and herbs and swirl until melted. Season with salt and serve immediately.

PESTO VARIATIONS

MAKES ABOUT 1 ½ CUPS

Pestos are great tossed in a pan of just-drained pasta with a pat of butter. Fold in some picked crabmeat or flaked smoked salmon for a more complete meal. Pesto is a wonderful accent for grilled, broiled, deep-poached, and slow-roasted seafood.

I've included some of my favorite pesto combinations here. To make any of them, follow this method: In this order, first place the garlic, then the oil, greens, and a pinch of salt in a blender. Blend until it becomes a smooth purée. Add the nuts and vinegar (if called for) and pulse until well combined but not super smooth. Taste and adjust the seasoning if necessary. Each recipe makes about 1½ cups. Pestos will keep in the refrigerator for up to 2 days.

ARUGULA PECAN

1 clove garlic

½ cup olive oil

2 cups arugula

Salt

¼ cup pecan halves or pieces

PARSLEY CASHEW

1 clove garlic

½ cup olive oil

2 cups flat-leaf parsley leaves

Salt

¼ cup cashews

1 teaspoon sherry vinegar

KALE WALNUT

1 clove garlic

½ cup olive oil

2 cups lacinato kale leaves, stems removed

Salt

¼ cup walnuts

1 teaspoon balsamic vinegar

ROUILLE

This sauce, which hails from the Mediterranean shores of Europe, is a traditional accompaniment to many seafood stews, but it's also delicious with grilled, slow-roasted, broiled, sautéed, or poached seafoods.

½ cup red wine vinegar

½ cup water or fish stock

½ cup slivered almonds

½ small onion, sliced

4 cloves garlic

1 red bell pepper, roasted, seeds and skin discarded

1½ teaspoons smoked sweet paprika

½ cup extra-virgin olive oil

Salt

Combine the vinegar, water, almonds, onion, and garlic in a small saucepan and bring to a boil. Boil until the almonds begin to soften, about 10 minutes. Remove from the heat and strain, transferring the solids to a blender and reserving the liquid. Add the roasted pepper, smoked paprika, and olive oil to the blender and process until smooth. Add some reserved cooking liquid, if needed, to thin the sauce to your preferred consistency, and season with salt. Rouille can be made and refrigerated up to 1 day in advance; return to room temperature before serving.

HORSERADISH LEMON MAYONNAISE

MAKES ABOUT ¾ CUP

Serve this mayonnaise with poached seafood, especially shellfish. It also makes for a nice dressing for crunchy vegetable salads and coleslaw.

½ cup Classic Aioli (page 257) or mayonnaise

2 tablespoons prepared horseradish

Juice of 1 lemon

Pinch of cayenne

Whisk together all ingredients. It can be made up to 3 days ahead and refrigerated.

GREEN GODDESS DRESSING

MAKES ABOUT 2½ CUPS

The best of both worlds—creamy *and* bright with herb—Green Goddess Dressing is wonderful over vegetables or as an accompaniment to grilled, broiled, slow-roasted, or deep-poached seafoods.

1 cup Classic Aioli (page 257) or mayonnaise

1 (2-ounce) can oil-packed anchovies

1 bunch watercress, trimmed

1 bunch tarragon, leaves only

½ bunch parsley, leaves only

Juice of 1 lemon

Salt to taste

Combine all ingredients, except the aioli, in a food processor and purée until mostly smooth and bright green. Let sit at least 1 hour and up to overnight to allow flavors to meld. Add the aioli and pulse to combine.

SIDES

A happy benefit of a seafood-rich diet is that such recipes pair well with a diverse array of vegetables. Because seafood tends to cook very quickly, prepare a few sides before you start on the fish. Many of these recipes can be made ahead (and even benefit from doing so). I suggest that you make one or two that are great served at room temperature, such as Fennel Coleslaw (page 272) or Asparagus with Vinaigrette and Mint (page 276). And then make one side dish that holds its heat, such as Seared Smashed Sea Salt Potatoes (page 274) or Rice Pilaf with Almonds and Fennel (page 288). The mix of textures, flavors, and temperatures can be so compelling that you might forget about the seafood.

ROASTED VEGETABLES
WITH PARMESAN AIOLI

SERVES 4

When spiked with anchovy and cheese, aioli comes to life in a whole new way. This simple sauce blooms under the heat of the roasted vegetables, beautifully complementing their sweet, rustic flavors.

2 pounds butternut squash, peeled, seeded, and cut into 1-inch pieces

1 pound carrots, cut into 1-inch pieces

1 pound parsnips, peeled and cut into 1-inch pieces

2 stalks celery, cut into 1-inch pieces

1 bulb fennel, including fronds, cut into 1-inch pieces

3 tablespoons extra-virgin olive oil

½ can anchovies (about 6 fillets), minced, oil reserved

Salt

Freshly ground pepper-allspice

3 tablespoons Classic Aioli (page 257) or mayonnaise

2 tablespoons grated Parmesan or pecorino cheese

4 scallions, chopped

1 teaspoon Worcestershire sauce

Preheat the oven to 450°F.

Combine the squash, carrots, parsnips, celery, and fennel in a large, heavy sauté pan. Toss the vegetables with the olive oil and the reserved anchovy oil. Season with salt and pepper-allspice. Roast in the oven until the vegetables are tender and golden, 20 to 25 minutes.

Meanwhile, combine the aioli, Parmesan, scallions, Worcestershire sauce, and minced anchovies, in a large bowl and stir together.

Remove the vegetables from the oven and immediately add to the bowl of dressing. Toss until evenly coated. Let cool to room temperature before serving.

PEPERONATA

SERVES 4

With its focus on sun-drenched Mediterranean vegetables, peperonata is kissing cousins with ratatouille. But its hints of deep sweetness and tang (from molasses and vinegar) put it in a league of its own.

¾ cup olive oil

2 stalks celery, cut into 1-inch pieces

1 bulb fennel, diced

1 large onion, diced

1 medium-hot pepper, such as poblano, Anaheim, or Hungarian, seeded and finely diced

1 (2-ounce) can oil-packed anchovies

1 butternut squash (about 2 pounds), peeled, seeded, and cut into 1-inch pieces

4 large ripe tomatoes, cored and chopped into roughly 1-inch pieces

3 tablespoons red wine vinegar

2 tablespoons molasses or maple syrup

Juice of 1 lemon

Salt

1½ cups water

Heat the oil in a wide, heavy stew pot, over high heat. Add the celery, fennel, onion, and pepper and cook for 5 minutes. Add the anchovies with their oil. Mash the fillets into the oil until they dissolve. Add the squash and toss to combine. Reduce the heat to medium and cook for 5 minutes.

Add the tomatoes, vinegar, molasses, and lemon juice, and season generously with salt. Stir to combine, and cook until the tomatoes begin to break down and release their juices, about 10 minutes.

Stir in the water and reduce the heat to low. Cover and cook until the vegetables are soft but not falling apart, about 30 minutes. Check the seasoning and adjust if necessary.

TRADITIONAL COLESLAW

SERVES 4

I always adore the first few forkfuls of slaw but tend to grow a tad tired under its unrelenting creaminess. This version, enlivened by a hefty dose of vinegar, holds your interest to the last bite. Salting the cabbage before adding the dressing removes some of its moisture and helps keep the slaw super crisp.

1 pounds cabbage, very thinly sliced (about 4 cups)

1 tablespoon salt

¼ cup red wine vinegar

2 tablespoons sour cream

2 tablespoons Classic Aioli (page 257) or mayonnaise

2 tablespoons chopped chives

Put the cabbage in a colander set over a bowl or in the sink, toss with the salt, and let sit for 20 minutes.

In a separate bowl, combine the vinegar, sour cream, aioli, and chives.

Gently squeeze the cabbage to remove any excess moisture. Add the cabbage to the dressing and toss to coat. Let sit at least 20 minutes (and up to 1 day) before serving.

CHILE-LIME COLESLAW

SERVES 4

My all-time favorite slaw. I eat it with anything and everything during the summer.

1 pound green cabbage, finely shredded (about 4 cups)

1 tablespoon salt

Juice of 2 limes

2 tablespoons peanut oil

1 fresh chile pepper, such as Fresno or serrano, very thinly sliced

2 tablespoons chopped cilantro

Put the cabbage in a colander set over a bowl or in the sink, toss with the salt, and let sit for 20 minutes.

In a separate bowl, combine the lime juice, oil, chile, and cilantro.

Gently squeeze the cabbage to remove any excess moisture. Add the cabbage to the dressing and toss to coat. Let sit at least 20 minutes (and up to 1 day) before serving.

FENNEL COLESLAW

SERVES 4

Fennel reigns supreme in my seafood cooking (for more about my obsession, see page 7). Its cool, crisp character is well complemented by the dressing's sweet vinegar and sexy herbs. If you don't have white balsamic vinegar, you can substitute ¼ cup white wine vinegar mixed with 2 teaspoons sugar.

1½ pounds fennel, very thinly sliced

Salt

¼ cup white balsamic vinegar

2 tablespoons sour cream

2 tablespoons Classic Aioli (page 257) or mayonnaise

2 tablespoons chopped chives

2 tablespoons chopped tarragon

Put the fennel in a colander set over a bowl or in the sink, season generously with salt, and toss well. Let sit for 20 minutes.

In a separate bowl, combine the vinegar, sour cream, aioli, chives, and tarragon.

Gently squeeze the fennel to remove any excess moisture. Add the fennel to the dressing and toss to coat. Let sit at least 20 minutes (and up to 1 day) before serving.

HUSH PUPPIES

MAKES ABOUT 2 DOZEN

Whenever I travel through the South, I seek out these crusty, aromatic balls of seasoned cornmeal. The best hush puppies I ever had were served at a restaurant in Reedville, Virginia. When I asked for the recipe, the chef came out and proudly announced that the mix came from a box. I've been trying to replicate the taste of those pups ever since. Here's my best attempt.

2 cups white cornmeal

2 teaspoons baking powder

½ cup grated onion

Salt

2 cups milk

1 large egg

Pinch of cayenne pepper

Peanut oil, for frying

Sift the cornmeal and baking powder together into a large bowl; set aside. Put the onion in a colander, season well with salt, and let sit for 5 to 10 minutes, allowing some of the juice to drain.

Transfer the onion to a bowl and add the milk, egg, and cayenne, whisking to combine. Add the wet ingredients to the dry ingredients, stirring until it forms a dough-like consistency.

Following the frying technique instructions on page 192, set up to deep fry at 375°F. Line a tray with paper towels.

Spoon 1 tablespoon of batter at a time in small batches into the oil, making roughly 1-inch-wide dumplings. Fry until golden-brown, crispy, and cooked all the way through, about 5 minutes. If the dumplings float on one side only, you will need to roll them over, using a slotted spoon, so that they cook evenly. Test one to see if it is cooked through and note the cooking time. Remove them from the oil and transfer the hush puppies to the lined tray to drain. Repeat with the remaining batter. Serve immediately.

SEARED SMASHED
SEA SALT POTATOES

SERVES 4

I love salt potatoes, a dish of new potatoes cooked in water so salty that they float. As the potatoes drain and dry, the salt crystalizes on their skins, weaving intricate patterns and splotches like a tie-dye T-shirt. I go one step further by smashing the potatoes in a hot skillet so that they loosely form a giant pancake, with one side crisp and brown and the other creamy. These spuds are equally delicious served piping hot or at room temperature with aioli on the side for dipping.

1 pound small red potatoes

½ cup gray sea salt (sel gris) or other sea salt—no need to use anything fancy

6 tablespoons extra-virgin olive oil

Place the potatoes in a medium pot with the salt and add just enough water to barely cover. Bring to a boil and cook until potatoes are easily pierced with a fork, 8 to 12 minutes.

Drain the potatoes well and let air dry for a few minutes. You will see a salt film begin to bloom on the skins, turning them into a beautiful marble swirl.

Heat the olive oil in a heavy skillet over high heat. When the oil is shimmering and just beginning to smoke, carefully add the potatoes and roll them in the oil to coat. Using a potato masher, crush the potatoes, pushing them together to form one big flat pancake. Reduce the heat to medium and cook, undisturbed, until the potatoes have developed a deeply crisped crust, about 10 minutes. Remove from the heat and invert a plate over the potatoes, one just larger that the pan. Protecting your hands with a towel, quickly flip the plate and pan to unmold the potatoes. Serve immediately or at room temperature.

ASPARAGUS WITH VINAIGRETTE AND MINT

SERVES 4

I really, really love mint. I use it with abandon in my cooking for two reasons: I love its flavor and the way it heightens and flatters just about any other ingredient, and it grows in my yard so prolifically that the only way to control it is to eat it with every meal. Hey, when life hands you lemons, make mint lemonade!

1 pound asparagus, trimmed

Salt

1 tablespoon whole grain mustard

1 tablespoon red wine vinegar

2 tablespoons extra-virgin olive oil

4 sprigs mint, leaves only

3 scallions, thinly sliced

½ cup good-quality olives

Briefly cook the asparagus in a large pot of boiling salted water for 45 seconds. Drain and spread the asparagus out on a serving platter to cool.

Whisk together the mustard, vinegar, and olive oil. Pour the vinaigrette over the asparagus. Tear the mint leaves into small pieces and sprinkle over the asparagus along with the scallions. Garnish with the olives.

ROASTED TOMATOES

SERVES 4 TO 6

As these tomatoes roast and dehydrate, they reduce in volume—and increase exponentially in flavor. It's worth making this recipe in bulk when summer tomatoes are abundant. I arrange any leftovers on a tray, separating them to keep them from clumping together, and freeze until solid. Once frozen, transfer them to an airtight container and keep in the freezer for up to 1 month.

2 tablespoons olive oil

2 tablespoons salt

1 tablespoon wine vinegar (sherry is my favorite)

1 tablespoon chopped fresh thyme leaves (from about 10 sprigs)

4 pounds plum tomatoes, halved lengthwise

Preheat the oven to 350°F. Arrange a roasting rack over a baking sheet.

Combine the olive oil, salt, vinegar, and thyme in a large bowl. Add the tomatoes and toss to coat. Place the tomatoes cut side up on the roasting rack. Bake until the tomatoes have become concentrated but are still supple (they should be easy to cut with a knife and fork, not chewy like a sundried tomato), about 3 hours (but start checking after 1 hour). Serve warm or at room temperature.

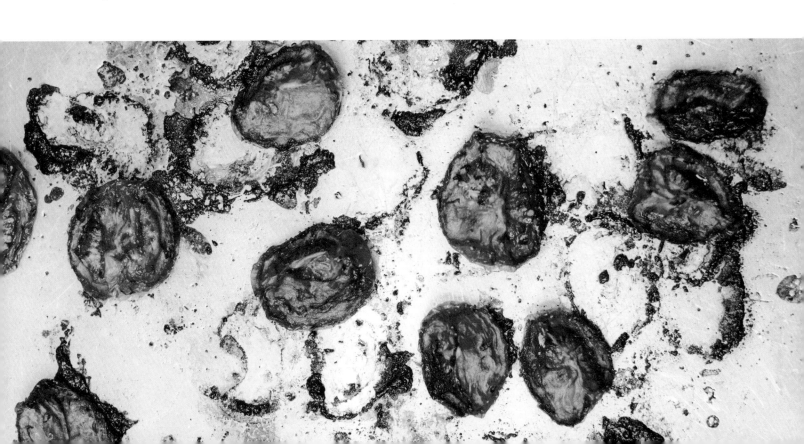

CILANTRO-LIME SWEET POTATOES

SERVES 4

I never boil or steam sweet potatoes without adding a little citrus to the mix. I love the way it (especially orange) transforms the sweets from a somewhat pedestrian ingredient into a showstopper.

1½ pounds sweet potatoes, peeled, cut into 1-inch cubes

Salt

Juice of 1 orange

Juice of 1 lime

2 tablespoons sesame or nut oil

3 tablespoons chopped cilantro

Boil the sweet potatoes in a pot of salted water with the orange juice until they are just barely cooked and still snappy to the bite, 10 to 15 minutes. Drain well, then immediately toss with the lime juice, oil, and cilantro. Let sit for at least 15 minutes for flavors to meld. Serve at room temperature.

CREAMED KELP

SERVES 4

Never tried kelp or other seagreens? Well, never fear—they are coming soon to a produce aisle near you. In fact, dried seagreens are already in most stores in the Asian foods section. Sugar kelp is a good gateway seagreen, as it is widely available and, when cooked, has a similar texture to kale or collards. In this recipe just a touch of cream brings out its nuanced, umami-rich flavor. For more info on the emerging North American seagreens industry, varieties, and sources, see page 139.

1 pod star anise

2 ounces dried sugar kelp (or 1 pound fresh or frozen kelp (aka kombu), drained and cut into bite-size pieces

1 tablespoon butter

1 onion, thinly sliced

2 cloves garlic, sliced

½ cup heavy cream or half and half

Finely grated zest of 1 lemon

Pinch of smoked sweet paprika

Pinch of ground mace

To rehydrate the dried kelp, add the star anise to a large pot of water and bring to a boil. Turn off the heat and add the kelp. Make sure to submerge it fully, pressing down on it with a spoon if neccessary. Let it soak for 15 minutes. Using tongs, remove the kelp and drain. Pat it dry. Tear the kelp into bite-size pieces and reserve. (The lightly flavored water is worth saving to use as you would a broth or stock in another application.)

Melt the butter in a deep, heavy pot over medium heat. Add the onion and garlic and cook until tender, about 5 minutes. Add the kelp and cook gently until warmed through. Stir in the cream, lemon zest, paprika, and mace. Bring to a boil, then remove from the heat and serve immediately.

CRUSHED CUCUMBER SALAD

SERVES 4

This juicy, spicy, crunchy salad makes an excellent accompaniment to grilled or broiled fish, especially richly flavored ones like bluefish and mackerel. The salad's heat blooms as it sits, so don't be tempted to up the spice. True fanatics can always add more at the table. Oh, and take care when smashing the slippery little cucumbers, as this operation can end up like that escargot scene in *Pretty Woman*.

2 Japanese cucumbers, trimmed and cut into 1-inch-thick rounds

2 tablespoons soy sauce

2 tablespoons rice vinegar or sherry vinegar

2 tablespoons toasted sesame oil

1 tablespoon fish sauce

1 teaspoon crushed red chile flakes

3 tablespoons Furikake (page 229), optional

Put the cucumber slices, a few at a time, in a large bowl, and use a potato masher or other heavy tool to crush them. This works best if you smash them on the round side of each slice, which gives roughly even pieces.

Add the remaining ingredients to the crushed cucumbers and toss until thoroughly combined. Let the salad sit for at least 10 minutes and up to 2 hours for the flavors to meld.

WILTED SUGAR KELP, COLLARDS STYLE

SERVES 4–6

My strategy for getting you to try kelp is to prepare it in ways with which you are already familiar. As the texture of rehydrated kelp is similar to the toothsome chew of collards, this revamping of a southern classic proves an easy sell to those who are suspect of seagreens. Smoky pork, sweet cider, a touch of chile . . . what's not to love?

¼ cup extra-virgin olive oil or butter

2 onions, halved and thinly sliced

3 garlic cloves, peeled

1 tablespoon crushed red chile flakes

1 pound meaty ham hocks or 6 strips smoked bacon

2 cups apple cider

2 cups water

2 bay leaves

Salt

4 ounces dried kelp (or 1 pound fresh or frozen seaweed, cut into 1-inch ribbons)

Heat the oil in a large pot over medium heat. Add the onions and garlic and cook, stirring occasionally, until softened, 5 to 7 minutes. Add the chile flakes and cook until toasted, 1 minute. Add the ham hocks, cider, water, and bay leaves. Season lightly with salt and bring to a boil. Reduce the heat to low, cover, and simmer until the ham hocks are tender, about 2 hours. (If using bacon, simmer for 30 minutes.) Discard the bay leaves. Remove the ham hocks and reserve.

Add the kelp to the cooking liquid, pressing to submerge it, and simmer until tender, 30 minutes to 1 hour, depending on the thickness of the kelp.

Meanwhile, remove the meat from the hocks and chop. Before serving, add the chopped meat to the pot and simmer gently to heat through.

COASTAL TABBOULEH

SERVES 4

Tabbouleh is such a refreshing dish. It's not often that something so satisfyingly filling is also brisk and lively in character. Here, I add crunchy wisps of wakame, a dried seagreen, to the mix of nubby bulgur and quinoa and an abundance of fresh herbs. Its briny, umami fun-time flavor makes this cool salad a knockout.

1 cup red wine vinegar, divided use

2½ cups water, divided use

½ cup cracked bulgur

1 cup quinoa, rinsed thoroughly under cold running water

1 ounce dried wakame
(for more info, see page 141)

1 tomato, cored and small diced

½ cup chopped flat-leaf parsley

¼ cup chopped mint leaves

¼ cup olive oil

Combine ½ cup of the vinegar and 1 cup of water in a bowl. Stir in the bulgur and let sit until tender, at least 1 hour. Drain and set aside.

Meanwhile, bring the remaining 1½ cups of water and the remaining ½ cup of the vinegar to a boil in a pot. Add the quinoa and boil for 15 minutes. Remove from the heat and let sit for 15 minutes. Fluff the cooled quinoa with a fork and refrigerate until chilled.

Combine the bulgur, quinoa, and wakame in a large bowl. Add the tomato, parsley, mint, and olive oil. Taste and adjust the seasoning if needed.

ZUCCHINI "SPAGHETTI" WITH GARLIC AND HERBS

SERVES 4

Shredding zucchini into long thin strands gives this modest summer staple an elegant twist. The key to its success is to shred the zucchini just down to the core, discarding the watery, seeded center (or saving the pieces for a vegetable broth).

4 to 6 zucchini (about 2 pounds total)

2 tablespoons butter

3 cloves garlic, thinly sliced

1 tablespoon water

Salt

1 cup chervil, leaves only

Either by hand or using a mandoline, finely julienne the zucchini, moving around the outside, leaving behind the seeded inner flesh.

Heat the butter in a large sauté pan over medium heat. Add the garlic and cook until translucent, about 3 minutes. Add the zucchini, water, and a generous pinch of salt, and continue to cook until the zucchini has wilted, releasing its juices and forming a nice sauce, 3 to 5 minutes. Add the chervil and toss to combine. Check the seasoning and adjust if necessary. Serve immediately.

AUNT GERI'S
NEW ENGLAND BROWN BREAD

MAKES 1 LOAF

Not long ago, my wife's father found a half sister whom he hadn't seen in many decades. With this reconnection came a delightful troop of new aunts, uncles, and cousins. How fun is that? At the family reunion, Aunt Geri brought out her time-tested recipe for this New England tradition, a deliciously moist bread made the old-fashioned way, steamed for hours in a coffee tin, which rings the bread with ridges, like a can of jellied cranberry sauce. There is something so very fun about connecting to your history, both on the plate and around the table.

1 cup bread crumbs

1 cup cold water

½ cup cornmeal

½ cup flour

½ cup molasses, plus more
for serving

1 rounded teaspoon baking soda

2 tablespoons butter,
divided use

Combine the bread crumbs and water in a bowl and let soak until completely absorbed, about 15 minutes. Add the cornmeal, flour, molasses, and baking soda, whisking until smooth.

Press the batter into a large coffee can, tamping down on it to remove any air bubbles. Place two layers of aluminum foil over the open end and secure it with rubber bands or kitchen twine. Place the can in a large deep pot and add enough water to come halfway up the can. Cover the pot and bring to a boil. Reduce the heat to medium to maintain a consistent simmer and cook for 2½ hours, checking the water level periodically and adding more boiling water if it gets low. Test for doneness by sticking a skewer into the middle of the bread. If it comes out clean, the bread is ready. If still doughy, cook another 20 minutes and test again. Remove from the pot and let cool.

When it is cool, remove the foil and puncture the bottom of the can to allow air in. Gently shake the bread from the can and slice into 1-inch-thick rounds.

Melt 1 tablespoon of the butter in a sauté pan over high heat. Working in batches, add the sliced bread and cook until crisped, about 4 minutes. Transfer to a low oven to keep warm. Repeat with the remaining butter and bread.

Serve the crisped bread with molasses or more butter, if you like.

RICE PILAF
WITH ALMONDS AND FENNEL

SERVES 4

Rice pilaf, a staple of seaside restaurants everywhere, has sadly lost some of its charm. But when made with attention and care, the combination of deeply toasted rice and almonds is spellbindingly fragrant and full of satisfying textures. Finishing the dish with mint is an unexpected twist, reminiscent of great Indian rice dishes. Pilaf is just as good—maybe even better!—eaten the next day.

5 tablespoons extra-virgin olive oil

4 ounces slivered blanched almonds

1 large bulb fennel, finely diced

2 cloves garlic, thinly sliced

2 cups basmati or jasmine rice

4 cups water

Salt

3 tablespoons chopped fresh herbs, such as mint or cilantro, plus more for garnish

Heat the olive oil in a medium saucepan over medium heat. Add the slivered almonds and cook until golden brown and very fragrant, about 5 minutes. Add the fennel and garlic and cook until the fennel begins to wilt, about 3 minutes. Increase the heat to high and add the rice, toss to coat with oil, and cook, stirring occasionally, until most of the rice has become toasted and well colored, taking on a variety of golds, browns, and charcoal (yes, burning a little bit is perfectly fine), 5 to 6 minutes.

Add the water and season with salt, then cover the pan and bring to a boil. As it comes to a boil, remove the cover and reduce the heat to low. Cook for 15 minutes more. Remove from the heat and let sit, covered, until the rice absorbs the last of the cooking liquid, 5 to 7 minutes. Add the herbs and fluff gently with a fork to mix. Serve on a large platter, garnished with additional fresh herbs.

ACKNOWLEDGMENTS

My beautiful wife, Carrie Anne
Katy Rivera
Michael Piazza
Cheryl Dahle & Future of Fish
The Dimin family
Josh Ritter
Steve Vilnit
Nick Branchina
Ben Martens
The Caggiano family
Jeff and Sandy Witherly
Aunt Geri Varney and family
Staub / Zwilling J.A. Henckels
Boos Block
Vitamix